Planet BB

The Boys' Brigade Around The World

Dave Chant

The Boys' Brigade prayer

Bless O God, The Boys' Brigade and give to it greater power to advance Your Kingdom throughout the world.
Grant in Your mercy, that every member, past and present may prove steadfast in his fight against evil, and true in his allegiance to you.
Help us in times of temptation; make us strong where we are weak; give us courage in difficulty; faithfulness in duty; loyalty in friendship; and finally, by your mercy, bring us into your everlasting Kingdom, through Jesus Christ our Lord,
Amen.

Planet BB

The Boys' Brigade Around The World

Compiled and edited by
David Chant

With help from members of the
2nd Sutton Coldfield Company

and Officers & Boys from all
'Around the World!'

Motto: **Sure and Stedfast.** Hebrews ch 6 v 19

Object: ***The Advancement of Christ's Kingdom among Boys, and the promotion of habits of Obedience, Reverence, Discipline, Self-respect, and all that tends towards a true Christian manliness***

www.planet-bb.co.uk

HiP
HISTORY INTO PRINT

HISTORY INTO PRINT
56 Alcester Road,
Studley,
Warwickshire,
B80 7LG
www.history-into-print.com

Published by History Into Print 2010

A CIP catalogue record for this book is available from the British Library.

ISBN: 978-1-85858-333-4

Printed and bound in Great Britain
by Information Press Ltd.

Contents

Acknowledgements

Without the help of the following, this book would have never got to publication. Aaron Gardner (Warrant Officer, 5th Scarborough, UK) has been my right-hand man since day one, and Sean Lai (Senior Cadet Lieutenant, 27th Singapore) my other right-hand man! Those two have been plugging the book and the Facebook group from its inception, and have written to people all around the globe. Thank you so much guys. You two are now known in half of the world! I could never have gleaned so much information from Asia without the help of 2 more right hand 'men', Janet Lim (1st Johor Bahru) and Michael Moorthy (President of Boys' Brigade Asia & Malaysia.). Not only did they produce articles for the book, but directed me to the best contacts all over Asia. I feel I know these 4 guys so well now – and I have never met them in the flesh! I am also indebted to Robin Bolton, President, Wolverhampton Battalion, and author of many a BB book for helping me out with the numerous gaps I was finding hard to fill.

To the following 'left-hand men', who have submitted articles to the book: Charlie Morris (Scottish National Director of Urban Saints: Glasgow), Paul Arkinstall, and John Pritchard (2nd Sutton Coldfield UK), Helen Ashby (1st Acomb, York, UK), Mollie Edbrooke (N Ireland), Barbara Lake (St Lucia), Al Henry (28th Leeds, UK), Nathanael Foong (60th Singapore), Walter Yee (BB Brunei), Tim Rogers (BB Queensland, and 46th Brisbane), Chiew Kin-Yan Darryn, Lt. Karnadi Lim, Chen Min (12th Medan, Indonesia), Jason Pheifer, Katie Nussbaum, Pat Kroiss, Olivia Boerschinger (Neenah, US), Okenwa Jideofor Nwatu (St Andrews, Fife & Enugu state, Nigeria), Maurice Williamson MBE (Chief Executive, Belfast Battalion), Sean Lai, Aaron Gardner, Stephen Cowden (Turning Point Chairman), Keith W Vinerd (DofE Manager, England and Wales), Wan Chang Da (1st Penang, Malaysia), Daniel Edmond So (BB38, Hong Kong), Janet Lim, Michael Moorthy, Anna Wells (BB Thailand), Thomas Moh (Reserve Lieutenant, 1st Sarikei, Malaysia), Les Bouterey (BBNZ President), Murray Donovan (Executive Officer, BBNZ/ICONZ), Adam Woodhouse (Youth worker, Bradford, and ex Captain 1st Hatfield), Neil Hawthorn (BB 7th Victoria Kerang & 1st Victoria Armadale), M.E. Hoare (author, Australia), Grace Wamala (Christian Children's Centre, Uganda), Colin Swinton (author History of BB Zimbabwe, 2009), Pang Seng Hock, BBAsia), Honorary Captain Lo Hoi Fook (Sarawak State Commissioner), Wei Ung (Sibu, Sarawak State), Philip Daley (National Director, Republic of Ireland District), Ben Phillips (1st Redditch UK), Priscilla Lee (40th Hong Kong), Pile Ray (9th Lusaka), Joshua Opolot (1st Kampala) Vic Russell (Global Fellowship).

A big Thank You to Paige Savage & Liam Dobson (5th Hull), George Smith & Joshua Lawrence (2nd Sutton Coldfield), for interviewing boys from overseas. And the interviewees, Calvin Leung (37th Hong Kong), How Kar Koh (39th Singapore), Evonne Hooi, & Tan Chan Yong (1st Johor Bahru), and Cheukling Aqua (Hong Kong), who kindly agreed to telling us about life in the BB in their countries.

Phillip Subrata, (Singapore), Michael Braithwaite (5th Hull), Sean Lai (27th Singapore) & Christopher Wall (2nd Sutton Coldfield) for help with designing the poster and logo. Tim Pennington (Web and Graphic Designer) who at the age of 16 produced our website www.planet-bb.co.uk.

Josh Lawrence and George Smith, joint 'Boy of the Year' seen here with Dave Chant.

A huge Thank You to all those who supplied photographs for the book (most of whom are already mentioned), and for all the hard work in seeking permission to use them.

Some guys have helped me in various ways over the months (apologies to all those I have missed out). They may not appear in the book, but their input has been a blessing. A few I can remember are: Jon Cole (Live sound engineer, E Yorkshire), Malcolm Turner & Steve Green (2nd Sutton Coldfield), Shawn Saimun Ang Kodrat (Singapore), for inspiring boys through the Facebook group, Mario Andreas (Indonesia), Lt Daniel So (Hong Kong), Kanardi Lim (Indonesia), Eddy Nara (HK74), Berner Ong (23rd Singapore), Albert Kwok (New Zealand), Tan Elim (Singapore), Tee Wei Sheng Simon (Singapore), Aik Ming (Malaysia), Andrew Ping Terng Eh (Singapore), Mario Andreas (5th Tanjung Morawa, Indonesia), David Sii (Sibu, Malaysia), Nikki Cartlich (Hull, UK) Denny Wu (Indonesia), Chris Chin (Malaysia), Resien Chiu (Indonesia) Tee Wei Sheng Simon (Singapore), Raymond Victor Lewis (UK). To all the 100s of Facebook 'friends' around the world who have kept me informed and amused for the past 18 months, and of course to my wife, Elaine, for putting up with me disappearing upstairs all year to work on the book, correcting my bad grammar, and letting me go to BB for the past 29 years of our marriage!

Lieutenant David Chant
October 2010

Foreword

I wonder what Sir William Alexander Smith would think if he were alive today? As I sit here in Glasgow, the home of The Boys' Brigade, I suspect he'd be amazed and perplexed. He never started an international youth ministry organisation, he never set out to change thousands of lives; he wanted to find a way to reach the older boys from his Sunday school class. And the success of his work has seen lives all across the globe touched and transformed.

I have enjoyed many years of involvement with BB in two continents, so wish all my fellow Boys and Officers my best wishes of support. I admire their dedication and commitment, week after week, putting in their best for often unseen rewards.

I started life in Boys' Brigade Australia never thinking it would take me as far, or have as significant impact as it has, in my life. I joined 15th Tas Launceston Company as a 10 year old half way through Number 1 (or Junior) Section in the early 1980's. As I was a long way behind the other boys my age in their badge work, I was put on an accelerated course to gain the badges other boys had in their first two years. I guess this spurred me on right from the start to work hard to achieve extra badges, which certainly helped later on.

My fondest memories are of the annual camp we ran each year, which was combined with our Girls' Brigade Company at a church member's farm. The kayaking was fun, the campfire jokes were awful, 'Poppa Peart's' famous stew was great (though I am still unsure about the jokes of dead possums in the stew) and the annual initiations. Having mostly repressed this

memory, I vaguely recall being dressed up in girl's clothing and having makeup applied. However, tying people to trees or hanging them in sleeping bags still brings a chuckle. I remember the officers still not believing this wild child at camp was the same mild, quiet, well behaved boy they saw each week; something within came alive at camp!

In 1987, by now an NCO, I attended the Pan Australian Camp in Adelaide, a national event with hundreds of boys. It was a fantastic time full of memories, sunburn and souvenirs. I think waking one morning after a storm and seeing the big top blown over and steel girders bent like melted plastic was amazing.

That same year my family moved city, so I joined 8th Canberra Company and found things very different. This Company only had a couple of committed officers, so the reliance on NCOs was much greater. I was teaching badge classes, leading drill squads and organising camps in no time. These years have been of great value beyond words as I learnt and developed leadership in challenging circumstances. The camps, the caving, the chaos! What a wonderful time we had. Racing against the clock to hand in all my badge work, I was privileged to earn my Queen's Badge in 1990, and had it presented by the Governor General in a very formal ceremony. That year I also went to the next PA Camp, this time in Brisbane, which was a different experience being one of the oldest boys there.

My last experience with BB in Australia was I had the honour of being a chaplain at a PA Camp in Canberra in 2002, which was a great delight and joy.

My journey in life took a very unusual turn in 2005, when a one way flight landed me and my family in Birmingham in England. To my delight, the church where we were Youth Pastors had a BB Company (2nd Sutton Coldfield), so I reconnected with BB, this time as the Company Chaplain (and as a BB parent!). My main objective here was to help the church see the BB as a vital part of its ministry and not just a group using our hall. This is where I met the author of the book you're reading, and he's a nice chap, even if he supports Aston Villa.

I cannot predict how my life would have been different if not for BB, but I know the massive impact it had on me as a child then teenager. The lessons in serving, leading, teamwork and being discipled I have learnt continue to be with me today, and as the Scottish National Director of Urban Saints, I need all the help I can get! I feel called to serve God in full time youth ministry, and am certain that my life in BB has been a huge part of this.

My congratulations for picking up this book, which is helping to bring the world of Boys' Brigade that one step closer together, as well as directing funds back into this global movement. So as we seek to advance Christ's Kingdom, my prayer is that more and more young people will come to experience life in all its fullness, as The Boys' Brigade continues transforming lives.

Charlie Morris

Introduction

Leading up to Christmas 2008, while others were searching the internet for those last minute presents, I was busy setting up a Facebook group with the aim of making it the biggest Boys' Brigade group in the world.

Within 3 months I had well over 1000 members from all corners of the world, and I was getting mail from NCOs, officers, Battalion Secretaries & Presidents, and each had a story to tell. It began to dawn on me that maybe there was a book in this somewhere. Photographs of BB Companies in far off exotic locations began to fill my Inbox, videos appeared, discussions began – soon it was clear that the book idea was becoming a reality. Amazingly the first publisher I contacted like the idea. How many times do we hear of authors having to traipse around dozens of publishing houses until a deal is struck?

Left to right: Ray Coombes, ex-captain 86th Birmingham BB Company; Betty Wilson, ex-1st Stafford BB Company; David Chant, 2nd Sutton Coldfield Company.

I decided from the beginning that all royalties would go to help BB Companies in a developing region such as the one in a small town in Ghana I feature in the book. No one has received payment for the pieces submitted – everything you see and read has been kindly donated. Royalty payments will go straight to *Global Fellowship* for their work with the BB overseas.

Two young officers have been in on the project from the beginning, Aaron Gardner of the 5th Scarborough, UK, and Sean Lai of the 27th Singapore. I cannot emphasise more strongly the help, dedication and encouragement these two have given me. Apart from their written contributions, they have cajoled others around the world to send in articles and photographs. All in the middle of exams at university! The Asia section has largely been made possible by the efforts of Michael Moorthy and Janet Lim of Malaysia. Towards the end of the project, I enlisted the help of Robin Bolton, President of Wolverhampton Battalion, and author of numerous BB books. Without his input the book would have had many more gaps than it undoubtedly has. These, and many others who have since become friends are listed in the acknowledgements.

I was stunned to find out that some Companies in the Far East and USA had over 600 members (one has 900!). One can only marvel at the photographs of these large Companies. But this book also includes Companies who are struggling to survive with only a handful of boys. These are also doing a wonderful job of Advancing Christ's Kingdom among Boys all over our planet.

It has proven impossible to get any information from some countries, particularly those in Africa and the Caribbean. The most common problem is lack of internet access. Every endeavour has been taken to include countries known to have BB. Sadly, a few countries that once had a thriving BB no longer appear to exist, including The Philippines where there are currently plans to reintroduce the Brigade.

People for whom English is their second language have written many of the articles and interviews. I have deliberately left much of the authentic text as it was sent to me in recognition of their hard work of producing their pieces in a foreign language.

I have endeavoured to avoid recounting a straightforward history of the BB in the individual countries, but rather have approached the task using a variety of voices. For the UK, for example, I have included a BB Youth Worker writing about his experiences, the Chairman of *Turning Point* in Northern Ireland tells us about a great annual event in the Province, the manager of the *Duke of Edinburgh's Award* for England and Wales explains how his work integrates with the BB, and there's a piece on the Boys' Brigade Memorial Garden from the man who had the vision for the project.

One of my favourite parts of the book contains interviews that took place via email between 3 boys in England, and 3 boys in Asia. A further interview features a girl from a UK Boys' Brigade interviewing another girl in Asia. Girls number more than 50% in a number of Boys' Brigade Companies overseas.

So, the hard work of producing this book is now over. It is therefore time to set about helping those in need in those distant places we in the West only ever hear about when disasters strike. Many areas within the 'BB World' are suffering from civil war, drought, and economic disaster. I intend to work closely with *Global Fellowship* to ensure any royalties from this publication will be used wisely. There is only one way this publication can help these struggling Companies, and that is simply to sell many copies. For every one that is purchased, the publisher pays a royalty payment. If every Company encouraged their boys, girls, and ex-members to buy an individual copy of the book this would raise many thousands of pounds. Inevitably some countries will not be able to afford copies. It occurs to me an individual might like to 'gift' a few copies to these regions. This can be done by contacting me via the website.

A quick word about who I am. I joined the BB aged 11 in 1966, when my parents informed me I was going to leave the Cub Scouts! I can't remember if that was under protest or not! By age 13, I was proud to be 'Boy of the Year'. I then moved steadily up through the ranks until I became an officer aged 18. I am still there to this day, some 40+ years on. My original Company (86th Birmingham) sadly closed in 1999, which led me to join the 2nd Sutton Coldfield, in Birmingham, England – the best BB Company in the world!

Lieutenant David Chant
May 2010. Worcestershire, England, the World!

The BB Grip

Have you ever wondered how the famous 'BB Handshake', used all over the world, came into being? Unfortunately I cannot tell you how it started but I can reveal how and when it came to Britain.

In August 1905, Rev. Joseph H. Cudlipp, Adjutant-General of the Pennsylvania Division of The United Boys Brigade of America, arrived in Liverpool on the start of a two month tour of the UK. He was editor and publisher of 'The Brigade Boy' the UBBA Journal and was accompanied by a Lieutenant, Sergeant, Corporal and Private of that organisation, described by him as 'Troop F'. In the previous year he had undertaken a trip around the USA with a similar group, but this was to be the trip of a lifetime.

Jos Cudlipp, who brought the BB Grip to the United Kingdom.

Jos Cudlipp admired the way in which the BB was organised in the UK. On his tour he visited most of the large cities in Britain and Ireland. Naturally, he was warmly welcomed wherever he went shaking hands with many British BB Officers & Boys. 'Troop F' was present for the Brigade Council weekend in Aberdeen and made a great impression upon its hosts, particularly members of the 1st Glasgow Company. The Founder's son G. Stanley Smith, then fifteen years old, observed that the UBBA members had a particular way of shaking hands known as the 'BB Grip'. The BB Grip was described as 'a handshake which involved dropping the little finger so that it goes between the little and third finger of the other chaps hand'. In a letter to 'Stedfast Mag' in 1957 Stanley Smith recalled the introduction of the grip... *'We at once adopted it in our own Company as "The First Glasgow Grip", I have no doubt other Companies did likewise. After I joined Headquarters Staff I travelled around a great deal and wherever I went I always used to pass on the handshake to Officers and Boys as "The BB Grip". It soon became famous and today it is known all over the BB world.* In some countries, such as Nigeria for instance, a slightly different extended version is used.

In the 1950s, Harold T. Barrow, former Company Chaplain and Secretary for Youth work in The Mission to Lepers, published a booklet entitled: 'The Boys' Brigade Handshake' being an extended version of a Bible Class talk he had given to the 1st Maidstone and 12th West Kent Companies. Using II Kings 10. v. 15 as his starting point. The booklet outlined the handshake as The Sign of Loyalty, A Declaration of Friendship, An Expression of Sympathy and Compassion, A Proof of Agreement, and A Covenant of Fellowship.

What does it mean to you?

Robin Bolton

Global Fellowship

It is the work of *Global Fellowship* that has been the main inspiration to me during the time spent working on PLANET BB.

The following extract from its excellent website will give you a taste of the extent of its work with youth around the world. It is to this charity that I have arranged the publisher to send the royalty payments to, as I know it will be safe hands.

I urge you to look at the website (www.globalfellowship.net), and to look for ways in which YOU can make a difference to the youth of our planet. There are many ways you can help. Becoming a helper or leader, join a mission overseas, make a donation, or even to pray on a regular basis for success in all they hope to achieve. Many of the countries featured on their website are the very ones that I have been unable to make contact with. So this fills in quite a few missing pieces for me.

Global Fellowship has grown into a vast network representing in excess of 750,000 young people spanning 60 organisations across the globe. The latest groups to seek membership within GF have included The Boys' and Girls' Brigade Burundi and Pathway Bangladesh.

Our first member was established over 120 years ago by Sir William Alexander Smith with the establishment of The Boys' Brigade in the United Kingdom (BBUK). In 1963 the international department of BBUK was replaced by The World Conference of Boys' Brigade. The objective of the new entity was to ensure that ownership and the decisions of BB were shared internationally, rather than under the jurisdiction of the UK alone. In 2002 the World Conference underwent a name change and became known as the Global Fellowship (GF) of Christian Youth. This change was to acknowledge the growing and diverse nature of youth organisations who desire to partner with us. While some work exclusively with boys and young men, others welcome boys, girls, teenagers and young adults from the age of 5 to 25 years.

I was sent the following to highlight current projects: (see website for regular updates of 60 seconds).

David

60 Seconds that mattered to Global Fellowship – June 2009

In April the ExCo of the Global Fellowship met in Copenhagen to consider the strategy and other business for the future.

Much was discussed and during the weekend, they had a meeting with Ulrich Piltoft of FDF Denmark and a very instructive talk from a professional web site developer.

From the meeting, amongst other items, it was agreed to look at restructuring the web site to make it more user friendly and hopefully capture a much wider audience; stage a special Global Fellowship Event on 28th November 2009 in Central London; look into ways to make it easier for our community to communicate with us, so as to share reports and photos of the many events happening around the world. ExCo are also considering ways of informing you of special events through your mobile phones and not just the web.

It is also planned to produce 60 Seconds monthly, therefore we will need more news of your country with photos where possible.

The ALC Junior Ministry India is planning a 30th Anniversary Camp. It will be held at ALC Community College Premises, Parangipettai this was to have taken place during the period 27th September – 1st October 2009 but had to be postponed.

If you require any further information then please contact E-mail: followthe star@sancharnet.in

Revd R. D. Vijayakumar, hitherto the Treasurer/ALC, was elected as the Sixth Bishop-President of the Arcot Lutheran Church by the General Assembly for the period 2009-2014.

The handing over of the post of the BB National Organizing Secretary for Cameroon took place on the 1st of May 2009 in the Musang Baptist church Bamenda at 11am. Henceforth all correspondences for the BB Cameroon are to be channelled to Rev. Njerou Paul Jumangong through this email address; njero_pa@yahoo.fr. We wish Paul every success in his new post.

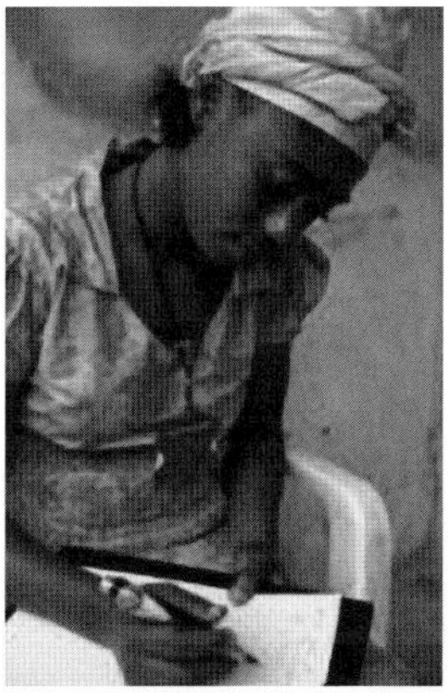

Leif visited Benin recently and spoke to Mrs. Loveth Mark of the 2nd Cotonou Company, Boys and Girls Brigade in Benin. She is working with girls from 6 to 8 years old.

She explains, "Some of them are coming from a bad and difficult background, I pray for the children and use the bible to guide them into a better life. I am also teach in the Sunday School."

Continue to pray for the Young Leaders' Workshop planned for August this year. We could still accommodate more young people. If you have not submitted names of suitable young leaders, 18 – 30 to your National Secretaries why not consider doing so?

Meet the 2nd Sutton Coldfield

Our Company has recently celebrated its first 60 years with a Thanksgiving Service at our Church St John the Evangelist, Walmley, Sutton Coldfield. Formed in 1948 our first Captain Mr David Holt was supported by the Reverend W A Weeks the vicar of the Church and a local Company the 29th Birmingham. Fund raising through such things as jumble sales allowed for the purchase of band equipment and numbers began to grow quickly. Many Boys came from the choir at the Church and the following year a camp took place at Abergele in Wales with 24 Boys.

Being part of the Birmingham Battalion has allowed us be involved in many activities and competitions particularly Band, Football, Table Tennis, Swimming, Athletics, Cross Country and Chess. We became Battalion Champions at Athletics in 2007 and 2008, Cricket in 1984, and Cross Country and Table Tennis on many occasions. In 1983 we came third in the National Chess Championships, which we hosted, from an initial entry of over 200 from the whole of the UK. We are also currently the proud holders of the prestigious Participation Trophy awarded to the Company in the Birmingham Battalion for most involvement in events and activities. The requirements of this trophy also include the Boys taking part in Church

1950s.

2007.

Birmingham Battalion Colours – and the symbol of our Facebook group
'Let's make this the Biggest Boys' Brigade Group in the World'!

1960s.

services, raising funds for a charity outside our organisation and producing a scrapbook of the past year.

Camp has been an important annual event mainly going to places in Great Britain, but in the past we have also travelled to Guernsey and Ireland, plus Holland and Germany for seniors camps. The early camps required use of the railway and equipment loaded at the nearby station including all tents, cooking utensils etc and even a piano. Boys had been known to travel with the equipment in the cattle truck.

We added the newest section 'The Anchor Boys' in 1992, now known as 'Anchors', and this has been a valuable addition to the Company. We have however been fortunate to have had dedicated Officers and Staff (not forgetting instructors, helpers and parents) and with the extra stability of only six Captains since we began – in order David Holt, Eddie Maddox, George Lawrence, Colin Russell, Bryan Perkins and presently Paul Arkinstall.

The achievements of individual Boys have been many including 1 Kings Badge and numerous Queensmen and Gold Duke of Edinburgh Awards. Although Boys & Officers leave to do many varied and different things when they leave us it is worth mentioning that Charlie Eaves and Suzanne Gregory both moved overseas to become missionaries.

The Company is still run on traditional lines but we aware that we must also change for the future whilst maintaining the importance of our object. Recent years have therefore seen changes to our class work such as local history, music appreciation, art etc. We have also started to introduce a different style of annual display.

With over 50 Boys in our care we are looking forward to what we can achieve over the coming years.

John Pritchard
Boy and Officer of 2nd Sutton Coldfield Company for 45 years

1960s.

2008.

The Belfast Battalion

The Belfast Battalion is the Founding Battalion on the island of Ireland and with 104 Companies and 5,600 Boys and Officers is the largest Battalion in the British Isles. It was formed in 1890, two years after the formation of the 1st Irish Company which is still active today in the St Mary Magdalene Church in inner Belfast where it was enrolled in 1888.

Some 15 full-time and part-time staff, under the direction of a Chief Executive, are responsible for the administration and running of the Battalion based both within the Belfast Headquarters offices in the City Centre area and the Battalion's Residential, Training and Activity Centre at Ganaway on the coast approximately 35 miles south of Belfast.

The prestigious and very attractive Belfast City Hall sits in its own grounds barely two blocks away from the Battalion offices and its walls are adorned with many portraits of former Lord Mayors who came through the ranks of The Boys' Brigade. Throughout its long history The Brigade has made a very big contribution to the social and community life of the city and is highly respected for its work with Boys and the contribution of Old Boys to the growth and development of the area.

As well as encompassing all of the Belfast County Borough area the Battalion covers the city and borough areas of four adjoining Councils – Castlereagh, Lisburn, North Down and Newtownabbey. Within this overall Greater Belfast Area the Battalion seeks to localise its work through five Groups based in South and East Belfast, North and West Belfast, Lisburn, North Down and Newtownabbey. In addition it has over the past decade operated a C.V.O. system of Company Visitation Officers whose brief is to help bridge any gaps between Headquarters and Company units on the ground.

Over the past five years the work of the Battalion and of its constituent Companies has been guided by a blue-print document entitled 'Target Excellence' and work is currently ongoing to provide a five year successor to this, starting in 2009/10. Quite a number of new initiatives and new programmes have emanated from 'Target Excellence' whilst a number reflect the Battalion's experiences during the severe period of civil unrest, best known as 'The Troubles', which affected Northern Ireland from the 1960s to the more relatively peaceful years at present being enjoyed by all sides of the Northern Ireland community. These were very challenging not to say dangerous years for many Boys' Brigade Companies especially in the inner-city areas but at no time did the B.B. put up any closure signs and Officers sought to operate 'Business as usual'.

At the beginning of each Session the Battalion Executive sets out a Statement of its Aims and Objectives for the coming year indicating, for example, that in '08 /'09 it would focus on key areas such as recruitment, young leaders, a new 5-year blueprint, the enhancement of

Company Programmes and the development of a less manpower-demanding Committee Structure.

Another key area earmarked for attention was the support and development of a Christian Outreach Youth Festival which was launched in 2007 by the Battalion. This is open to B.B. members and other youth organisations for the age group 11 – 18 and now extends across Northern Ireland organised by a dedicated young Management Team no longer drawn just from Belfast but from other Battalions and youth groups. Almost 300 were present at the April '09 Festival which took place at the Ganaway Centre and immediately following which all the indoor bedspaces were booked out for 2010.

Among the more recent new initiatives and programmes of the Battalion have been:

- The launching of a Back-to-Basics Good Citizenship programme to bring home to B.B. members the common courtesies of life and good social behaviour backed up by attractive and informative leaders manuals and young people's pocket-sized guideline cards
- A Drugs Awareness programme delivered to local units in 6-week modules
- A C.E.O. in Action programme providing Challenge, Enjoyment and Opportunities to young people and aspiring leaders based on a wide range of outdoor and indoor activities
- A Cross Community / Good Relations programme majoring on the benefits of A Shared Future for all the people of Northern Ireland regardless of culture, race or creed
- A Fit Futures programme giving Anchor Boys and Junior Section Boys a full appreciation of the merits of keeping fit and healthy through fun activities combined with healthy eating.

One of the most successful programmes provided by the Battalion and led by a full-time Sports Development Officer has been a B.B. Broncos Multi-Skills Coaching Games and Activities Scheme which is now annually taken up by hundreds of B.B. Boys.

Shepherd's Lodge Cottage.

All these programmes are heavily augmented by a very full and vigorous range of training courses including .....

- Company Section Discover Workshops and Child Protection
- Captain's Element residentials
- Queen's Badge Leadership and Completion Courses
- One-Night Training Events
- Holiday Leadership Courses.

As part of or in addition to the above the Battalion operates

- the Ganaway Activity Centre which offers 100 indoor bedspaces, mostly in en suite accommodation ..... 2 lodges ..... a country cottage ..... a Millennium Centre (which also includes 2 Sports Halls, a games area, training rooms, an indoor climbing wall, badminton courts etc.) ..... a Church for up to 160 people ..... crazy golf ..... outdoor climbing and zip line ..... low level and high level Ropes Courses
- the Shepherd's Lodge Mountain Centre sleeping 34 people with adjacent camping facilities
- a 20-acre Centre of full-size and 5-a-side and 7-a-side football pitches
- a full-scale retail shop which supplies the needs of Companies throughout Northern Ireland and well beyond.

This is but part of the story of the Belfast Battalion which seeks to base its Christian work on what it calls the three 'I's – Imagination, Innovation and Initiative.

Maurice Williamson M.B.E. Chief Executive

Turning Point

Turning Point is a Christian youth festival for young people aged 11 – 18 held at the Ganaway Activity Centre, Millisle, Northern Ireland. It is organised by a dedicated Management Team consisting of leaders from The Boys' Brigade and other youth organisations, and we are currently organising our third annual event. Turning Point is generously supported by a number of agencies, including BBUK. Turning Point takes place during the last weekend of April. The theme this year was *Identity* and we were all challenged as Rick Hill took us on an interactive discovery. Our new house worship band Heart *Ablaze* led us in praise.

Our programme this year saw the return of popular features, and some brand new activities. We had The BackBeat Café, The Live Lounge playing host to many events such as SingStar Superstar, Games Arcade, the Big Quiz (Christian Aid), *Guitar Hero*, Cinema, *Christian Aid* Tent with their delicious fair trade chocolate brownies, *Tearfund* Prayer Pod, *Open Doors* prison cell, dance sessions, cookery, artist workshops, craft sessions, BBQ, sports-hall games, hockey, football, crazy golf, tag rugby, volleyball and much, much more! The Trading Post was also a popular venue, offering exclusive *Turning Point* hoodies, beanies and t-shirts, book stall, novelty items and *Open Door's* campaign shoe laces.

Many of the activities at Ganaway (archery, climbing wall, high and low level rope courses and the zip line) were all in full swing for those attending the weekend to enjoy. Our counselling team also ran an energetic social on the Friday night as well as sumo wrestling and giant twister. The activity programme was rounded off on Sunday with a huge water fight, complete with water balloons, hose pipes and soapy water slide.

In addition to our young people's programme, we also had events for group leaders. A number of local agencies displayed their youth work programme materials to help equip leaders with new resources and skills to help them develop their important work with their groups.

The aim of *Turning Point* is to "provide an active festival style weekend that will be inclusive of all young people aged 11-18; that will incorporate Christian teaching and worship through a modern approach that will appeal to and be relevant to today's young people; and that will promote and encourage the development of a personal Christian faith". We believe that *Turning Point 2009* has once again fulfilled its purpose, and through our whole programme Christ's Kingdom has been greatly advanced not only among the young people present, but also the group leaders and volunteers.

On the Sunday morning we always have a session to allow the young people attending the weekend to give us their honest feedback about the weekend and to tell us what they want to see in their programme next year. They also provided really useful ideas for us to include in the programme for Turning Point 2010. I am also delighted that four young people took the opportunity to volunteer as part of our Management Team for next year.

Other exciting news to note is that by lunch time on the Monday after Turning Point, all the indoor accommodation for next year was booked and we now have groups putting their names on a waiting list – what an encouragement! If you would like to be part of a future Turning Point – either bringing a group along or volunteering – please contact us: office@turningpointni.org.uk

Stephen Cowden *Turning Point Chairman*

€25,000 for the Laura Lynn Children's Hospice Project

As part of the 125 celebrations The Boys' Brigade in the Republic of Ireland chose The Laura Lynn Children's Hospice Foundation as its national charity.

The 'Laura Lynn Children's Hospice' Foundation was set up in 2001 as a result of an enormous personal tragedy in the lives of Jane and Brendan McKenna which saw them lose both of their precious daughters Laura and Lynn in the space of just two years.

Their youngest daughter Laura was born with a hole in her heart, and having endured and survived six months and two serious operations, went on to have a few relatively good years, with the final repair operation to come. Sadly when it did, Laura did not survive it and she died in 1999, aged just 4. Her mum describes Laura as 'a very happy, funny, beautiful little girl. A real Shirley Temple with her mass of curls, she always had a smile and made us all laugh so much – she was so cute and so brave'.

Lynn, on the other hand, had 13 years of perfect health until she was diagnosed with Leukaemia on the very day her younger sister passed away. How she coped with her illness, her adored sister's sad death and her own impending death was an inspiration to her parents.

Jane says "Lynn had a wonderful 3 weeks in which she knew she was dying, wished it could be different, but accepted it with dignity, aged just 15. She had great courage and huge acceptance. She lived every minute of those weeks to the full, which is how we should all live our lives. She taught us how to live and how to die. It is why we are where we are, and why we survive. The hope of the Laura Lynn Hospice Foundation is to help those families, whose children have life-limiting and/or life-threatening conditions, and are coping at present with limited support."

The Hospice or House, as Jane prefers to call, it will be located in the grounds of The Sunshine Home in Leopardstown, it will be about respite for the family as a whole. Its concept is about putting '**Life into a child's day, not days into a child's life**'. For parents, it will give that much needed break – often as simple as a decent night's sleep. It will also support healthy siblings, who are very much left out, when a sick child needs 24 hour care.

Killian Dunne, 1st Portarlington Company – Mr. Alex Thackaberry, District President – David Rohu, 1st Greystones Company – Rev. Derek Sargent, District Chaplain – Harry Steacy, 1st Littlewood Company – Mr. John Young MBE, Brigade Hon. Vice President – Mrs. Jane McKenna, Laura Lynn Foundation – Mr. Philip Daley, National Director ROI District.

It will offer ongoing support for the family when the child has passed on, for as long as they choose, which is hugely important, as life can never be the same again.

During the year Companies throughout the District have been working tirelessly to raise much needed funds for the Laura Lynn Hospice Foundation. There have been cake sales, sponsored walks, sponsored cycles, making and selling Christmas cards, quizzes a concert hosted by the renowned International Soprano Niamh Murray and collections at various services throughout the District to raise funds for this project.

The District were delighted to present Jane McKenna of the Laura Lynn Children's Hospice Foundation a cheque for €25,000 at our recent Annual Founder's Service in St. Ann's Church, Dublin.

Meet Aaron Gardner, Worship Leader – a typical young BB officer?

Read about Aaron's strong faith, and the work he achieves within his Company, and with other local Churches. He also recounts his time at Firm Foundations, and the BB Tattoo. Aaron's Company, the 5th Scarborough, is in the North-east of England.

I have always had an interest in the Bible and the word of God. I always sat listening intently to our various Reverends on a Sunday parade service, and once old enough, attended the normal Sunday morning services.

I decided to take the next step in my faith, Baptism in June of 2005 and did it in true Boys' Brigade style during a monthly parade service. The day went really well and the warmth of fellowship in the church was felt by many.

After ten years continuous service to The Boys' Brigade, in June 2009 I decided to become a member of my church by being confirmed. Again the service was held on a Boys' Brigade Sunday parade with many young people in attendance.

I find working with children highly rewarding, and also feel children in this current millennium don't seem to be respected, and people are quick to place a stereotype on them.

Being a young worship leader within The Boys' Brigade, I use the following verse taken from 1 Timothy 4:12 (*The Message* Bible), to demonstrate that although I am young, it is God's will that I teach young people about the Kingdom of Jesus.

"Get the word out. Teach all these things. And don't let anyone put you down because you're young. Teach believers with your life: by word, by demeanour, by love, by faith, by integrity. Stay at your post reading Scripture, giving counsel, teaching. And that special gift of ministry you were given when the leaders of the church laid hands on you and prayed—keep that dusted off and in use."

Also every child is unique similar to a fingerprint and has to be cared for in different ways.

Jesus said *"Let the little children come to me, and do not hinder them, for the kingdom of heaven belongs to such as these."* This small but very powerful verse is exactly what youth workers should do, let the word of Jesus reach out to them and develop a new generation of Christians and give a fresh look to what can be sometimes called an old church.

My experiences with young people

I have had an eventful journey of faith with young people to date; this miniature article explores some of the tearful, exciting and powerful moments.

Achievement

Most Boys' Brigade display nights are the same but May 2008 saw the promotion of nearly all of our current Anchor Boys. I had started my leadership role within my Company as a Corporal with this group of Anchor Boys and from the age of five my fellow Boys' Brigade friends and I had helped to teach them skills such as crafts which promotes their gross and fine

Aaron gets his Queen's Badge July 2007.

motor skills, games which promotes their gross motor skills and team work skills, and finally worship which teaches them an understanding of God's kingdom.

To see them make the great achievement of moving up into a new section and to also see them throughout the 2009 session using the skills taught both at Boys' Brigade and school is just truly fantastic! Also as much as it was a great achievement for them, it also gave me a great sense of pride. But I always put this aside and concentrate on the young people and how they feel about their achievements.

Powerful

Prayer during Youth Fellowship

During 2007 I started to attend my Church's Youth Fellowship meetings for secondary school aged children as a member, but due to the heavy work at college I had to stop attending. Late 2008 after completing college and a summer work contract, I decided to return as a leader. This was probably one of the wisest decisions I have ever made.

Most Sunday evenings we pass the Bible around and pray for someone important, something important or just anyone who needs a prayer. The first time I did this as a group the feeling was just overwhelmingly awesome. Some Sundays we also play games like 'Dodgeball' this is a great way of making conversation and finding out what stimulates the youth of today.

Following on from Youth Fellowship there are more young people attending the Sunday evening service, although this is less than ten and it would be fantastic to see more.

Exciting & Adrenaline pumping

Working with young people is constantly exciting. Over the past five years I have been involved in voluntary work with children, not once have I not enjoyed it. The reason I chose to add the word 'adrenaline pumping' to the heading is because it's a perfect analogy when describing young people. They are the ignition that gets the adrenaline pumping through youth workers' bodies and once it's pumping it should never stop.

Recently during an Anchor Boys session I had a spare five minute slot to do a relay, I had 'Follow My Leader' in mind then decided to add a rather crazy twist. Please note, you need a fairly large hall to do the running part of this game, although don't worry if your hall is small, I've devised a mini version which is just as exhausting.

I lined the lads along the wall at the end of our hall and explained the rules:

When the music plays you must run to the end of the hall and back, but you must also copy anything I do. So if I hop there and back, you must hop too. Then when the music stops you've got to copy 'exactly' what I do, so if I sit down then you've got to sit down. The slowest person to complete this part of the game has to sit out. When I asked them if they understood the rules I received a rather loud and enthusiastic 'YES!' back.

Well, I have never felt so much adrenaline run through my body before. They enjoyed the game so much we played it five times, the amount of energy was amazing and I was shattered. Due to the lack of oxygen getting to my brain we decided to play the game in a circle. Keeping the same rules as the running game, just do it in a circle instead. Although I would recommend getting a NCO to lead this game unless you feel super fit because it's a very intensive game.

Kingdom Faith

Recently I went to a *Kingdom Faith* meeting in my local library. At first I was cautious because I didn't know what it would be like.

When I got there I was greeted by fellow Christians and shown the various rooms within the library that they use. I was introduced to the youth worker there and some of the children.

Being used to a Methodist service I expected an organ, but there wasn't one in sight, just a massive worship band (from all ages and backgrounds), and modern instruments. For the first forty minutes the worship band played 'jazzed up' hymns and the young people in attendance were up at the front hopping around and singing passionately which I thought was truly awesome. I couldn't resist but joining in. After the worship band had played the introduction music the children went into a smaller room where I and some fellow youth workers followed. The children's group was called 'J24-7' which stands for 'Jesus 24-7'. I was blown away by the amount of faith among them and the interest they showed when the Bible story of 'The Good Samaritan' was read was just truly amazing.

Following the visit I have decided to become a 'Kingdom Faith' youth worker and be a part of their fantastic team – alongside my BB work of course!

Firm Foundations 22nd to 25th May 2009

This year, our Company, the 5th Scarborough had a combined *Firm Foundations* trip with 1st Market Weighton. We left our church at 3 o'clock to collect the lads and lasses from Market Weighton.

After a long 5 hour journey we arrived at Feldon Lodge, head quarters of the Boys' Brigade, and home of *Firm Foundations*.

The weekend was jam packed with games, camping and fellowship to a whole new level.

This year, the organisers split the two worship venues into a 'boys only' and 'girls only' worship zone on the Sunday night. During worship in the boys' tent, the Holy Spirit could be felt. Then near the end of the worship time the people leading the evening invited young people to the front to take the next step with God. At first I was cautious whether the young people would take this step in such a public way, but to my amazement over 40 young people were up the front with me.

The power of prayer was immense; I and a two young people from Plymouth got into a 'rugby scrum' and prayed for each other in silence, but could feel the Holy Spirit there guiding us.

After such an amazing and emotional evening for some, every lad on site was left speechless. People that weren't too sure about their faith were looking for answers, and Christians that had never taken that step before were filled with the Holy Spirit along with the boys that were looking for answers.

The final worship session of the weekend on the Monday morning was Holy Communion. This symbolic event within Christianity was a fantastic opportunity for young people to learn the greatest event within the Bible, the death and resurrection of Jesus Christ.

Within my circle we did our own mini Communion service, the young lad I prayed with the evening before did a prayer for the wine, and I did a prayer for the bread. Then at the end we got into another 'rugby scrum' while sat down then to my amazement after the prayer we learnt that all the people in our circle, apart from me were from the same Town of Plymouth.

Overall the weekend was amazing and I look forward to the future years of *Firm Foundations*.

The Boys' Brigade Tattoo

25th April 2009 at Braehead Arena, Glasgow.

Our Company, 5th Scarborough left at 9am on the Saturday, heading for Glasgow.

The first leg of the journey to Scotch Corner was sweaty due to the very hot weather. Once parked at the service station we ate lunch, and some, like me paid extortionate prices for coffee and biscuits. After Scotch Corner, the next stop was Glasgow. Fellow Companies from our Battalion and District who were taking part in the band section of the Tattoo were already there. Once in Glasgow we checked into a *Travel Inn*. The rooms were very basic, but just what we needed for a good night's sleep.

The Tattoo was truly amazing; it showed exactly what The Boys' Brigade does to be a helpful and active partner in a young person's life. There were separate sections demonstrating various activities within the Brigade, including Gymnastics which I thought had died out when the badges were altered in the 60s.

There were also the bagpipes which are rarely played below the Scottish border. This section to me was the best by far, the talent needed to learn the bagpipes alone is amazing, but then to have the lungs to hold out some of the notes at eleven years old plus just blew me away.

At the end of the Tattoo all the sections, Company Colours, and old members gathered together. This clearly demonstrated that The Boys' Brigade isn't a dying organisation but a 'growing' one!

After the Tattoo, we returned to our rooms and chilled. I decided to make a cup of coffee but the kettle had other things on its mind like trying to electrocute me. I got a replacement kettle which didn't work, and finally at midnight I got a working kettle but couldn't be bothered to make a coffee so went to bed!

Overall the event and journey to and from Glasgow was a memorable one!

Tribute to Aaron

Having an encounter with Aaron Gardner is like opening a well-shaken bottle of lemonade. He froths, bubbles and effervesces his way through every moment of life, his joy of the Lord spilling over and touching everyone he meets.

Aaron's faith has been developed and tested by many struggles and difficulties. He knows that it takes a lot of lemons to make the best lemonade. Because he's been there, and knows that Jesus has walked beside him, he's able to share that assurance with others. The members of the Boys' Brigade couldn't be in safer hands than his. His caring compassion for each child shines bright, and each one is surrounded by a level of prayer and deep pastoral concern that is second to none. His beaming smile and non - judgemental acceptance of all, draws both boys and leaders to him. If you want to see the absolute love of Jesus in action, seek out Aaron, evangelising, caring for and accepting whoever God puts in his path.

He's an excellent cook, knows all the best campsites and builds a wicked spaghetti and marshmallow tower, too...

Elizabeth Stanforth-Sharpe

The Duke of Edinburgh's Award, United Kingdom

In 1956 a scheme known as The Duke of Edinburgh's Award was started which provided progressive activities for young people from the age of fourteen. The Boys' Brigade appreciated that this could complement our existing badge scheme and were actually involved in the pilot schemes for the Award in the United Kingdom as early as 1955 and have taken part ever since. Over the years many young men, and now girls, have undertaken the Award, now known as The DofE, at Bronze, Silver and Gold levels alongside Boys' Brigade awards and it has been particularly relevant to members doing The Brigade's highest award, the Queen's Badge, for which many of the requirements are similar to the Silver Standard of The DofE.

The age range for DofE has changed over the years and is currently available to young people between the ages of fourteen and twenty-five. There are three levels – Bronze, Silver and Gold – and there are four Sections at each level, some of which have recently changed their titles and are now known as Volunteering, Physical, Skills and Expedition. The Volunteering Section calls on young people to make a difference within their communities by giving service to others, the Physical Section encourages greater physical fitness and a healthy lifestyle, the Skills Section seeks to develop personal interests and the Expedition Section encourages a spirit of adventure and discovery by completing a journey as part of a team. At Gold level only there is an additional Residential Section which offers personal challenges in a residential setting with previously unknown colleagues.

In 2006 The Duke of Edinburgh's Award celebrated its 50th Anniversary. The Boys' Brigade formulated a personal message of greetings to Prince Philip which was despatched by the Brigade President from our Annual Brigade Council in Cardiff and carried in relays throughout the country by DofE participants to be finally presented to His Royal Highness personally at the Anniversary Celebrations in Edinburgh some eight weeks later by three young members representing England and Wales, Northern Ireland and Scotland.

DofE continues to flourish and is of considerable help in retaining Seniors in The Boys' Brigade. Some of the activities followed are constant and traditional and others are regularly updated to keep abreast of the fluctuating interests of the age group.

Keith W. Vinerd
DofE Manager (England and Wales)
The Boys' Brigade

The Boys' Brigade Memorial Garden

The idea of a Boys' Brigade memorial garden came to me after attending the opening of the Church Lads' and Church Girls' Brigade Garden at the National Memorial Arboretum at Alrewas in Staffordshire.

Contact was first made with Paul Kennedy (who manages the Arboretum) during the Christmas period 2005, where he gave us an idea of the various sizes of gardens and how much the plot would cost and what we could and could not do.

The proposal for a Memorial garden was put to the Birmingham Battalion who said that they would support it at the next West Midlands District meeting. All the members of the West Midlands District supported the proposal and a steering group was set up with the West Midlands District President as chair and representatives from all the constituent members of the district being Birmingham, Worcestershire, Mid-Staffordshire, Wolverhampton and North Staffordshire.

A plot was offered to the steering group in early 2006 which we accepted because it was situated just outside the chapel and next to the Church Lads' and Church Girls' Brigade Garden. After a site meeting, the steering group put together several ideas and suggestions and an artist's impression of what the garden could look like was produced. This was then presented to the Arboretum for approval and comment.

Being happy with the plan, an appeal was launched at Brigade Council in Cardiff, 2006 and this was received very well. By the end of the weekend we came away with the £3000 funding required to pay for the plot and the promise of a 10ton block of Ailsa Craig granite for our memorial stone. Over the following months as the project became better known, the donations started coming in, not only in financial terms but promises of materials and labour.

The steering group gave another presentation at the 2007 Brigade Council meeting at Bradford, giving details of the progress to date, and to acknowledge the gifts that we had received during the previous year.

Work on the garden started in early 2007 with the construction of the soakaway, retaining wall and leveling of the site. The slate monolith was collected from Wales, the granite boulder was collected from Scotland, and both were delivered to the garden. Also a large slab of Portland stone was delivered from the quarry that was producing all the stone for the National Armed Services Memorial. All the landscaping, positioning of the memorial stones and paving were professionally laid. The twin Bog Oak pillars from The Republic of Ireland and Northern Ireland were placed at the entrance to the garden.

Volunteers dug a small trench round the perimeter of the garden and put some good quality soil in them to plant the box hedging, then some 10 tons of top soil was spread over the garden. Two areas were prepared for the planting of Boys' Brigade roses. Later the turf was delivered and again a small team of volunteers laid the turf and planted 125 each of daffodils, tete a tete daffodils, pheasant's eye narcissus and grape hyacinths. The garden was almost finished, it only remained for the slate monolith to be hand carved with the Boys' Brigade Object and have its metal plaque fitted. The bench was placed on the Portland stone, which by now had the words 'Sure' and 'Stedfast' carved at each end.

The official opening of The Boys' Brigade Garden was held on Saturday 20th June 2008. A short service of thanksgiving was held at the Arboretum Chapel by the Rev. Professor Alan Main, the former Brigade President, and the opening was conducted by the current Brigade President Sir Kenneth Calman.

On July 5th 2009, a time capsule was buried in the garden containing 125 objects connected with Boys' Brigade; this is to be opened in 2059. A finishing touch to the garden was the placing of a piece of stone over the capsule location from Pennyland House the birthplace of the Founder Sir William Smith.

Website: www.memorialgarden.boysbrigade.org.uk.

Paul Arkinstall
Captain of the 2nd Sutton Coldfield Boys' Brigade Company

S/Sgt Liam Dobson of the 5th Hull Company interviews S/Sgt Tan Chan Yong

How have you found being part of a global organisation?

Great, because I get to meet people from all around the world and gain more exposure.

Have you had any experience of other countries ways of doing things in The Boys' Brigade?

Yes, but only via my Band tour to Thailand once only...

My Company (5th Hull) goes on holiday to France every 2 years, what are camps like at your Company?

We have our Company Camp almost every year in the jungle. We have overnight picnics at the beach.

I've been in 3 different Companies (2nd Scarborough, 5th Scarborough & 5th Hull) how many Companies have you been part of, and if it's only one, how long have you been a member?

Nope. I have never been a member of any other Company... I am still in the same Company, the 1st Johor Bahru in Malaysia.

Does your country have battalions and districts similar to our country? And if yes do you have events within them such as competitions?

Yes! We have "Pesta" (Festival) almost every 2 years. Normally we have fellowship and games through it, and of course every time we have band competition, drill competition, singing competition and this coming pesta we will have some new competitions, such as website design and others. In fact it will be held in Penang.

What has the response been like from your friends and family to you being in The Boys' Brigade? Are there any situations where you have felt intimidated because of people's thoughts towards the Brigade?

At first my family objected because they felt that I was involved in too many activities, but now no more complaints because I have managed to balance my life in family, BB, studies and work. No. I never felt intimated, but I feel proud to be a BB member.

If you could change one thing about your Company what would it be, and why would you do that differently?

The "Last Minutes Attitude". I would like everyone to work together and not wait for each other, to initiate the task at hand. I also hope we can instil more Christian values to our members.

Why did you become a member of The Boys' Brigade in the first place? Is it because you joined when you were young and it has just become a regular thing, or you joined through friends? If you joined through friends, when you were a bit older, did you get on with the other members quickly?

Yes. I joined BB when I was young and this has already become a part of my life. I do not know whether I would be able to get on with the members, if I had joined BB when I was a bit older, but I think it should not be a problem because I am an extrovert.

What is your fondest memory of The Boys' Brigade and what made it such a memorable time?

When we won the Championship, in the Inter-Platoon Drill Competition 2007, because it brought back my Platoon's morale.

Being an older member of the brigade do you have many responsibilities, and how do you overcome dealing with younger members?

Of course everyone will have a lot of responsibility, but since I am not in school anymore, seems lesser. I try to mix with my younger members by having meals with them and spending time with them after BB or after school.

Our highest badge in the Brigade is the Queen's Badge, what is your Badge system like and what achievements do you have?

Our highest badge is Founder's Badge while the second highest is the President's Award. I haven't achieved much. Still far from achieving the President's Award.

We have girls in our Company and it works great. Do you have girls in your Company? What are your views on having girls in the organisation?

We do have girls. Nowadays, in my Company, the girls are more active than the boys. Of course it works great too!

S/Sgt Tan Chan Yong
1st Johor Bahru Company
The Boys' Brigade in Malaysia

Sgt. Paige Savage of the 5th Hull Company interviews Sgt. Evonne Hooi of the 1st Johor Bahru Company

What is it like being a girl in the Boys Brigade?
I think it is good for girls to be in BB, as girls can participate in the same activities as the boys. Girls can gain more knowledge but there are also some boys that look down at girls. They think that there are some things that boys can do, that girls can't do.

Why did you choose to join the BB?
Very exciting! There are many special events going on all year round. You can learn new things & gain knowledge. Everyone is just like one big family. People in the BB are friendly.

What has been your best experience?
Company camp 2007. It rained heavily, that resulted in the water level rising and we were forced to break camp early and go home. In the process of breaking camp, everyone had to follow the Officers' instructions; we all did our best to work as fast as possible. Although the situation was chaotic, everything was completed in a short while. It was an unforgettable memory for me.

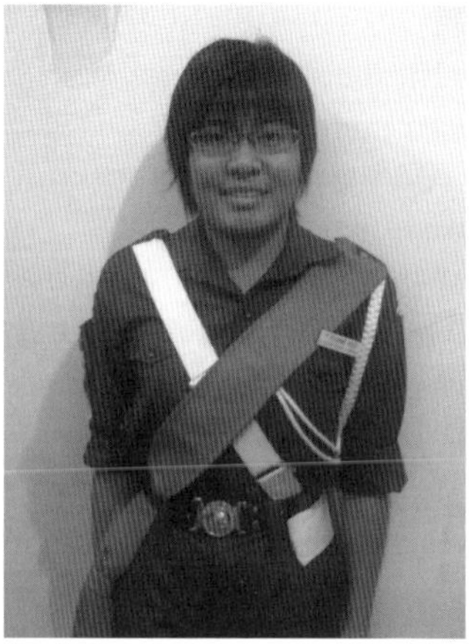

If there was one thing you could change about your Company what would it be?
Boys and girls should be treated the same.

Are there many girls that are involved within BB in your country?
Yes. But there are some Companies that don't have the Girls' Wing.

In England the girls in the BB fully participate in every activity, is it the same there?
Yes.

We have lots of different competitions like Band, Football, Drill, Hiking, and swimming, what types of competitions do you do, and are there any you would like to do?
I participated in Band and Drill competition, and I would like to play football and go hiking.

When I take part in BB events I am treated like 'one of the guys' and I'm not treated different because I'm female, is that the same for you?
Yes, for some events only. Some of the girls in our Company are treated as "guys" but most aren't.

The Boys' Brigade has helped me a lot in my life, has it helped you become a stronger person and do the lessons you learn at BB give you any life skills you wouldn't get alone?
Yes. Serving others and treating & loving them as your family members. Also the importance of communication.

I feel very welcome and everyone I meet all seem so friendly. I feel like I belong to a bigger family, do you get the same feeling? Are you an NCO and if so what responsibilities do you have?
Yes. Being a bridge between the Officers and members. Helping others to solve their problems. Taking care of juniors. Not only matters that are related to BB but also in their daily life. (Helping them to change and become better persons)

Sgt. Evonne Hooi
1st Johor Bahru Company The Boys' Brigade in Malaysia

We asked Cheukling Aqua from Hong Kong

What's it like being a girl in The Boys' Brigade?
I really not a good writer..... (specially in English)

Actually, I can share something ...... for you.

I don't know... it seems as a boy like.... we don't have any difference in our meeting every week.

We have our lesson, drill, read the bible & pray all together. When we at camp, just finish all our task together......

Just equality of boys & girls..... And sometime you can see the girls are stronger than the boys......

Ling

This is The Boys' Brigade Asia

The Formation

Purpose

BB Asia has been formed out of a desire to maintain the unity, purpose and specific character of The Boys' Brigade everywhere. It came into being to give The Boys' Brigade an international organisation which would advance its growth, interest and cause.

Objects

The objects of BB Asia are:

- to promote the development and extension of The Boys' Brigade to new fields and territories.
- to strengthen the work of The Boys' Brigade internationally and within each member country
- to help its members to develop and adapt their respective programmes to the needs arising out of the conditions in which young people live and work
- to develop sympathy, understanding, and cooperation among all its members.

The Initiation

On 7 May 2002, at the East Asia Regional Fellowship meeting held in Bangkok, Thailand, the idea of BB Asia was first mooted and a Pro-tem Committee formed under the chairmanship of Mr Michael Moorthy, the Brigade President of BB Malaysia. The paper proposing the new international confederation came from Mr Lim K Tham of BB Singapore.

BB Asia was officially inaugurated on 26 July 2003 in Johor Baru, Malaysia when BB representatives from Hong Kong, Indonesia, Malaysia, Singapore and Thailand signed a memorandum of agreement giving birth to the regional association.

Membership

BB Asia's total membership as at 31 December 2008 stands at 30855 comprising of 8 countries in our membership – Brunei, Hong Kong, Indonesia, Macau, Malaysia, Philippines, Singapore and Thailand.

THE BOYS' BRIGADE
ASIA

Meetings

General Council Meetings

GCM is held once in two years. Each country is allowed a maximum of 6 representatives. At this meeting Country Reports are presented, some common issues discussed and the Executive Council elected.

Executive Committee Meetings

ECM is conducted twice a year at different venue each time selected by the committee.

The Executive Committee 2009-2010

At the 5th General Council Meeting, the following persons were elected and/or appointed as office bearers.

Position	*Name*	*Country*	*Local Position*
President:	MR MICHAEL MOORTHY	BB Malaysia	President
Vice-President I:	MR SUNNY WU	BB Hong Kong	Chairman
Vice-President II:	COL (Rtd) TAN KOK HENG	BB Singapore	President
General Secretary:	MR LIM K THAM	BB Singapore	
Hon Treasurer:	MR TYE YEW MENG	BB Singapore	Brigade Secretary
Members:	MR ONG TEONG HOON	BB Singapore	Vice-President
	MR ALBERT CHING	BB Singapore	
	MR SAMUEL CHOO	BB Malaysia	Vice-President
	MRS RESIEN CHIU	BB Indonesia	Vice-President
	MS EVA KONG	BB Hong Kong	Executive Member
Chaplain:	REV DR LI-PING KWONG	BB Hong Kong	President
Associate Chaplain:	REV RICHARD TOK	BB Malaysia	Chaplain

1st BB Asia Academy in Camron Highlands, Malaysia.

Secretariat

Full time staff: Mr Lawrence Tay, Executive Secretary.
Website is: www.bbasia.org
Email address is now: secretariat@bbasia.org.
Official correspondence address is 5 Jalan Anak Gasing (6/5), 46000 Petaling Jaya, Malaysia.
Bi-monthly newsletter is ACROSS ASIA.

Programme

BB Asia Academy

This Academy is a training course opened to all BB members 18 years and above in Asia and other parts of the world. The objectives of this program are:

- Interaction and Fellowship
- Exchange of Programme Ideas & Skills
- Inspiration for Ministry
- Better Understanding of BB Ethos & Spirit

2nd BB Asia Academy in Bogor, Indonesia.

Development Plans

2009-2011

I. REGIONAL EXTENSION

Extension to new countries

- **Nepal**
- **Nagaland, India**
- **Mongolia**
- **Myanmar**
- **Taiwan**

Strengthening of existing work

- **Cambodia**
- **Indonesia**
- **Macau**
- **Philippines**
- **Thailand**

II. TRAINING & EDUCATION

- **To develop pool of trainers**
- **To organise BB Academy**
- **To hold staff development conferences**
- **To assist in organising courses and be available to conduct training**
- **To create interest in and ownership of the BB Asia and initiate opportunities for educating the Fellowship on the work of BB Asia**

III. COMMUNICATIONS

- **Website**
- **Newsletter – both electronic and printed forms**
- **Occasional In-house circulars**
- **Corporate Brochure**

IV. FUND RAISING

- **Projects**
- **Friends of the BB Asia scheme**
- **Sponsors scheme**
- **Donor database**
- **Church Support**

V. PUBLICATIONS & RESOURCES

- **"About BB Asia"**
- **Profile of BB Countries**

VI. DEPOT & EQUIPMENT SUPPLIES

(1) **To coordinate co-production of BB equipment**

(2) **To produce BB Asia badges, collaterals and souvenir items**

(3) **To market and handle sales of the above**

VII. YOUTH EXCHANGE & MISSION DEVELOPMENT

(1) **To promote and coordinate youth exchange among member countries**

(2) **To build up commitment to missions**

(3) **To encourage partnerships among churches and BB units**

History of The Boys' Brigade in Malaysia

The Boys' Brigade did not come to Malaya until the after the Second World War. A British soldier by the name Robert Davis (former Captain of 6th Birkenhead Company at the Tranmere Freehold Methodist Church and later Tranmere United Reformed Church) gave the idea of The Boys' Brigade to one of Penang's great educationist, the late Mr Geh Hun Kheng, who accepted the challenge to be the first BB Captain in Malaya.

Mr Geh realised that he had to do his "small share" to win the Boys over from the various subversive groups that were so rife after the Pacific War.

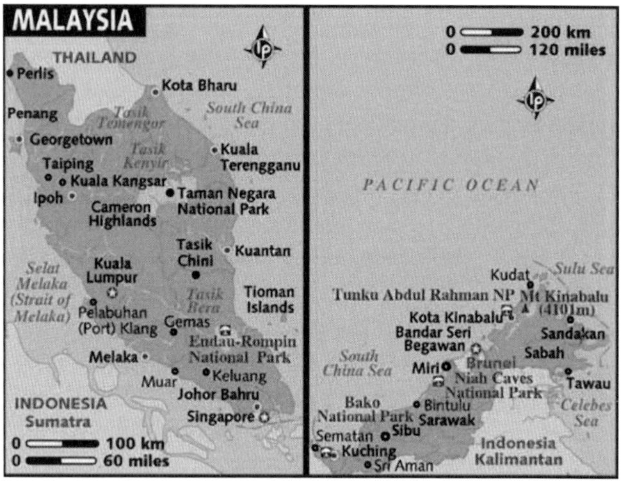

The first meeting of 20 Boys was held in the Methodist Church in Madras Lane on a Sunday in September 1946.

Penang thus became the springboard from which Companies were started first in Kuala Lumpur and then in other parts of the country. When Malaysia achieved independence on 31 August 1957, The Boys' Brigade was given the honour of being invited to take part in the Merdeka Parade (Independence Day Parade).

After Merdeka (Independence), The Boys' Brigade began to spread rapidly as a result of the formation of the Malayan Council of The Boys' Brigade under the initiative of Mr Khoo Oon Soo. More and more Companies were founded in every major town in Malaya. Even small rural towns began to have BB Companies functioning efficiently.

By this time firm and friendly contact had been made with the BB in Singapore which helped in the supply and sale of equipment and with the founding of the first Company in Borneo in 1959, the 1st Kuching Company.

In 1962, the BB in Malaya became a member of the Pacific Regional Fellowship (subsequently joined the East Asia Regional Fellowship when it was formed later) and the first Pacific camp was held with the co-operation of the Singapore Battalion in Port Dickson in December 1963.

On 5 December 1964, the former Federation of Malaya Council of The Boys' Brigade, the Singapore Battalion and the 1st Kuching Company merged into The Boys' Brigade in Malaysia.

With the political separation of Singapore from Malaysia, The Boys' Brigade in Singapore ceased to be a component District of The Boys' Brigade in Malaysia as on 19 August 1965.

In Malaysia, the National Council began to establish Companies in Sabah and Sarawak, maintaining friendly ties with the BB in Singapore.

The development of The Boys' Brigade in Malaysia took a revolutionary turn when it invited girls into its membership. It was first introduced in 1989 and debated for a few years before experimental measures were approved in 1992. The move received favourable response and strong support from churches and individuals.

The starting of the Girls' wing was to cater for the girls in a locality where a Girls' Brigade Company did not exist, & also where there was a shortage of volunteer manpower. Today, more than 20 Companies in the BBM have girls in their Membership Roll, and many girls have been appointed NCOs, and they have proven to be capable, & adapting well to the activities of the BB. Since 1992, The Boys' Brigade in Malaysia has also begun to play a more significant role in the extension of BB work in the East Asia Regional Fellowship, including conducting training and support for the BB work in countries like Indonesia, Thailand and the Philippines.

Today, there are over 70 Companies spread throughout the length and breadth of Malaysia. Since the setting up of a BB HQ in 1989, a permanent building has been purchased, and currently staffed by a team of 5 full-time personnel.

The Boys' Brigade in Malaysia has come a long way since 1946. Many things have since changed; many youth had come and gone through the ranks. Throughout all these years, the BBM has been able to hold on to its Object and continue in serving the youth of Malaysia.

As the nation is fast moving towards greater heights in development, it is believed that the BB shall be called on to play an even greater role in the development and training of the Malaysian youths. (Partially extracted off the BBM Website: www.bbmalaysia.org)

Michael Moorthy
President of Boys' Brigade Asia & Malaysia

How the BB came to Malaysia (then Malaya)

Wan Chang Da

This story illustrates how BB came to Malaysia through the formation of First Penang Company, narrating from the perspective of Reverend Khoo Cheng Hoe, the first Chaplain of First Penang Company. All facts are gathered from "The First Penang Story", published in *First Anchored in Penang* (2006).

Revd Khoo Cheng Hoe and his wife.

The Japanese had surrendered. The war is over.

What a blessing that my family had once again gathered for dinner. During a conversation over the meal, I raised my concern about the rampant delinquency of teenaged boys in church. As Pastor of the Madras Lane Chinese Methodist Church in Penang as well as father to ten young boys, this social issue was always close to my heart.

Then one of my sons, Oon Teik, who was studying medicine in Singapore prior to the war, shared about an organisation called "The Boys' Brigade" that he came across in Singapore. Oon Teik explained that this organisation was somehow similar to the Boy Scout movement, which was quite established in Penang. However, apart from instilling discipline in the boys, I was told that what made BB unique was, in fact, the foundation of this movement which was anchored upon Christian values.

I was excited about the idea and immediately asked Oon Teik to write to Mr James Fraser in Singapore about starting the Boys' Brigade movement in Penang. Mr James Fraser was the founder of BB in Singapore. A fortnight later, a parcel came back containing enrolment posters and pamphlets about BB. We are now better informed and very excited to kick-start this exciting initiative.

At the church's Local Church Executive Committee, I proposed the idea about starting the BB movement. Driven by the need to reach-out to Boys as well as the promotional materials we received from Singapore, the committee agreed to the idea of the Boys' Brigade, which eventually was sponsored by the English-speaking congregation of our church.

The next task was then to "hunt" for leaders to lead the movement. We approached Mr Geh Hun Kheng, the Headmaster of the Anglo Chinese Primary School (ACPS), to be the

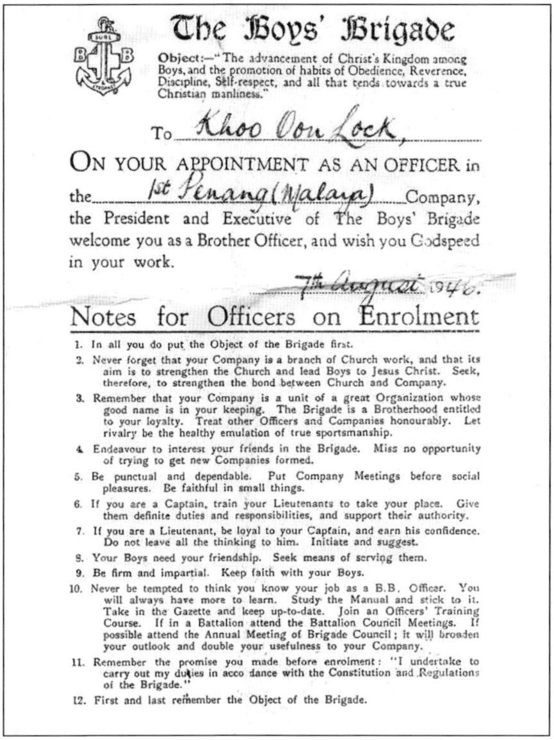
The Boys' Brigade

Object:—"The advancement of Christ's Kingdom among Boys, and the promotion of habits of Obedience, Reverence, Discipline, Self-respect, and all that tends towards a true Christian manliness."

To Khoo Oon Lock,

ON YOUR APPOINTMENT AS AN OFFICER in the 1st Penang (Malaya) Company, the President and Executive of The Boys' Brigade welcome you as a Brother Officer, and wish you Godspeed in your work.

7th August 1946.

Notes for Officers on Enrolment

1. In all you do put the Object of the Brigade first.
2. Never forget that your Company is a branch of Church work, and that its aim is to strengthen the Church and lead Boys to Jesus Christ. Seek, therefore, to strengthen the bond between Church and Company.
3. Remember that your Company is a unit of a great Organization whose good name is in your keeping. The Brigade is a Brotherhood entitled to your loyalty. Treat other Officers and Companies honourably. Let rivalry be the healthy emulation of true sportsmanship.
4. Endeavour to interest your friends in the Brigade. Miss no opportunity of trying to get new Companies formed.
5. Be punctual and dependable. Put Company Meetings before social pleasures. Be faithful in small things.
6. If you are a Captain, train your Lieutenants to take your place. Give them definite duties and responsibilities, and support their authority.
7. If you are a Lieutenant, be loyal to your Captain, and earn his confidence. Do not leave all the thinking to him. Initiate and suggest.
8. Your Boys need your friendship. Seek means of serving them.
9. Be firm and impartial. Keep faith with your Boys.
10. Never be tempted to think you know your job as a B.B. Officer. You will always have more to learn. Study the Manual and stick to it. Take in the Gazette and keep up-to-date. Join an Officers' Training Course. If in a Battalion attend the Battalion Council Meetings. If possible attend the Annual Meeting of Brigade Council; it will broaden your outlook and double your usefulness to your Company.
11. Remember the promise you made before enrolment: "I undertake to carry out my duties in accordance with the Constitution and Regulations of the Brigade."
12. First and last remember the Object of the Brigade.

Officer's appointment letter.

Captain. Given his vast experience as an educationalist as well as an elder in the church, he is more than qualified to provide leadership to this organisation. Praise God, he agreed.

I then recalled that perhaps a friend who was the Chaplain in the Reoccupation Allied Forces might be able to provide us with some "connections" of capable people to be part of this initiative. Mr Robert Gordon Davis and Mr John Pudney were introduced to us. Mr Davis, formerly Captain of 6th Birkenhead Company, was instrumental in the recruitment. He gave an introductory talk over Radio Malaya and a speech about BB in the school. Besides Mr Davis and Mr Pudney, we also got Mr Ho Weng Hong and three of my sons, Oon Lock, Oon Hoe and Oon Eng, to be part of the team.

At the first meeting, 35 boys registered. That was a good start. The officers organised numerous activities for them. They went on a cycling tour, a swimming trip at an abandoned tin-mine, a picnic by the beach and a Talent-time Night.

On 20 July 1946, we received a letter from the Boys' Brigade Headquarters in London, acknowledging the registration of First Penang Company. We were now officially part of the BB family! With this, we proceeded to organise the first official ceremony of the Company, the Enrolment Sunday.

First Official Photo, November 1946.

first penang company
60th
honouring GOD's faithfulness
anniversary
SURE
&
STEDFAST

First Penang Company, 60th anniversary.

Captain Geh Hun Kheng.

It was such a joy that on 7 August 1946 during the Enrolment Service, I had the honour of presenting the appointment letter to the Captain and four officers as well as enrolling the Boys as official members of the First Penang Company. Three months later, we took the first photograph as a Company. I was there with eleven officers and 47 boys.

What began as an idea a year ago has now become a reality. The Boys' Brigade has anchored in Penang.

History of 1st Johor Bahru Company

The Boys' Brigade in Malaysia

1st Johor Bahru was officially enrolled on the 4th November 1956 under the wings of The Singapore Battalion who helped in the formation of the Company. The founding Captain was Mr. Michael Ang who was assisted by Rev. Dick Shad as Chaplain, Mr. Joseph Victor and Mr. Tony Joyce as Officers.

In 1965, the Company struggled without a Captain. It was a critical time, in the life of the Company. However, we are thankful to S/Sgt Yap Yok Foo and S/Sgt Ong Eng Boon from 1st Kluang Company, for their assistance. In 1966, both Mr. Paul W. Juby and Mr. Gan Yan Guan from 1st Sungei Petani Company, was transferred to Johor Bahru, due to work commitments, and assumed the position of Captain and Officer respectively. The total commitment and dedication from both of these men helped the Company grow in strength and commitment. Many new ideas and systems were introduced, by Mr. Paul. Many boys found Jesus as their Personal Saviour during the late 1960's. Mr. Paul Juby showed his qualities as a fine and dedicated leader. He diligently sent weekly personal letters to all the Boys in the Company, and had also created the "BB Pews" in the church during Church Services on Sundays.

In 1967, a Bugle Band was formed. Instructors from the British Army that was stationed in Johor Bahru, taught the Boys. In 1968, the Band took a big step of courage, in making the decision of participating in the National Band Competition. We came out Fifth, out of the total of six bands, in our first attempt. Bagpipes were then added to the Band, in 1971.

Isaac Chua, Koh Kelvin and Kumar Doraisamy.

In 1974, Mr. Paul Juby had to return to England. The position of Captain was then taken over by Mr. Michael Moorthy, a boy that grew up through Rank & File, under Mr. Paul Juby's leadership. He has since been at the helm except for two short intervals.

Mr. Michael Moorthy has recently stepped down from the position of Captain of 1st Johor Bahru, and effective from 1st March 2009, Mr. Jason Chong has taken over the position.

Mr. Michael Moorthy is currently the President of both Boys' Brigade Asia & Malaysia.

Edited by Janet Lim

The BB Singapore Story

Early days in Singapore

1st Singapore Company, 1933

James Milner Fraser, founder of BB in Singapore, was a member of the 23rd Aberdeen Company and an officer in the 23rd London Company. He came to Singapore as a young architect, and was a town planner by profession. He contributed not only to the physical infrastructure of Singapore but also the moral development of the many Boys in his time.

The 1st Swatow Company was established in the Chinese city of Swatow. A mammoth Company of 300 strong and most efficient. It survived for many years till the communist regime forced many of its members to flee to Nanyang to escape persecution.

There was a link between Swatow and Aberdeen. A Swatow Old Boy, SGT Quek Eng Moh, recognised James Fraser from his BB buttonhole badge and told him that the ex-Swatow stalwarts wanted to start a Boys' Brigade Company in Singapore. Together, they founded the 1st Singapore Company at Prinsep Street Presbyterian Church on 12th January 1930, fulfilling Fraser's pledge to his ex-captain to pioneer a BB Company.

When the Company was officially enrolled in August 1930 by Brigade Headquarters in London, membership was 40. Singapore was represented at the Jubilee Celebrations in Glasgow in 1933 by Choy Ah Soo and Tan Keng Kang, final year students in school.

By 1936, the Singapore Battalion was 200 strong. Fraser served as Battalion President from 1936 to 1956. In 1940, he handed over captaincy of the 1st Singapore to one of his Boys, the redoubtable S P Chua.

The War Years & Post War

BB activities had to be suspended in the Second World War during the occupation of Singapore by the Japanese Armed Forces (Feb 1942 - Sep 1945). Some of the Officers and Boys remained fervently loyal to The Boys' Brigade; and Company records were preserved at great personal risks. The proud Singapore colours were burned and the drums brought back by the Jubilee Boys were stashed away in the store of Prinsep Street Presbyterian Church to await liberation. Fraser himself was a prisoner of war and worked on construction of the infamous Burma Railway.

After the war in 1945, S P Chua revived the 1st Singapore Company. He was joined immediately by James Milner Fraser and by 1950, the Battalion had regained its old glory.

Our Patron, Membership & Endorsements

There are more than 7000 Officers and Boys in 117 BB Companies in Singapore, each of which is attached to a school and co-sponsored by a church. Such schools include Singapore

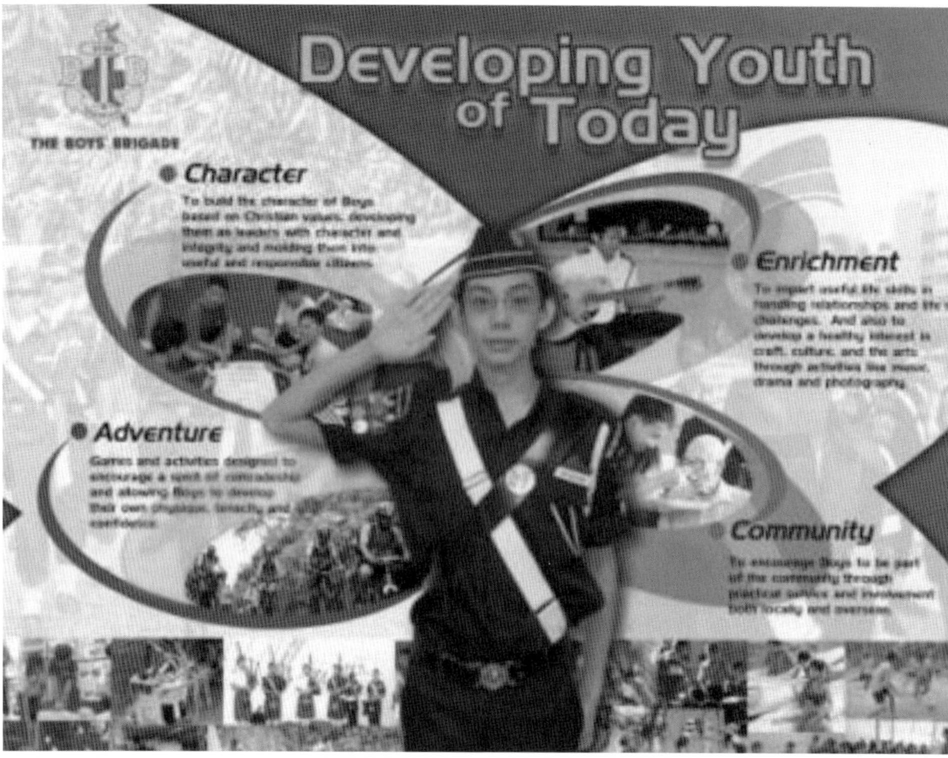

Polytechnic, Raffles Institution, Pioneer Secondary School, Victoria School, Anglo-Chinese School, Henry Park Primary School, Tao Nan School, Rosyth School and St Hilda's Primary School.

In Singapore, The Boys' Brigade has the distinguished patronage of His Excellency, the President of the Republic.

The BB is endorsed by the Ministry of Education as one of the Uniformed Youth Organisations in schools. We are a member of the National Council of Social Service and the National Youth Council. The Boys' Brigade is also gazetted as an institution of public character and is registered as a charity under the Charity Act 1982.

BB Singapore Honoured

On 12 January 2000, 77 Prinsep Street, where Prinsep Street Presbyterian Church stands, was marked as the 41st Historic Site of Singapore by the National Heritage Board to commemorate the 70th Anniversary of The Boys' Brigade in Singapore.

The Boys' Brigade in Singapore has its very own flower. "Dendrobium The Boys' Brigade" was named on 18th September 1999 in celebration of our 70th Anniversary in Singapore. The flower symbolises the aspiration of BB youth, and reflects a new generation with the best hybrid of courage from our heritage and boldness to face the future.

Year	*Milestones*
1930	The 1st Singapore Company at Prinsep Street Presbyterian Church was founded with 40 members.
1936	The membership of Singapore Battalion grew from 40 to 200. Fraser also served as Battalion President in the year till 1956.
1940	Fraser handed over the captaincy of 1st Singapore Company to one of his Boys, S P Chua.
1942-1945	BB activities were suspended during the Japanese Occupation. Records of BB Companies were preserved at great personal risks where some of the Officers and Boys who remained fervent to BB lost their lives.
1945	After the war ended, S P Chua revived the 1st Singapore Company. He was joined immediately by James Milner Fraser and by 1950, the Battalion had regained its old glory.
1951	The King's Badge was started as the highest award in the Seniors Section.
1954	The King's Badge was renamed Queen's Badge with the coronation of Queen Elizabeth II.
1962	The Queen's Badge was renamed Founder's Badge. Still the highest and most honourable award for Senior Boys, achieving the Founder's Badge was the goal of every BB Boy.
1971	The Brigade was honoured to have the President of the Republic of Singapore as its Patron.
1983	BB Singapore celebrates the Centenary of the founding of The Boys' Brigade in 1883, Glasgow, United Kingdom.
1988	With the aim of spreading joy and cheer to the less fortunate during the Christmas season by collecting gifts, The Boys' Brigade Sharity Gift Box was started with a collection of 7000 gifts. The Sharity Gift Box theme "Have a Heart Share a Gift" clearly states the project's objectives.
1990	BB celebrates its 60th Anniversary. Camp Temasek was initiated to encompass campers from other Uniformed Groups and BB from other countries.
2000	BB celebrates its 70th anniversary. Prinsep Street Presbyterian Church, where the 1st Singapore Company was founded, was marked as the 41st Historic Site of Singapore by the National Heritage Board. BB also had an orchid, Dendrobium Boys' Brigade named after her. BB CARES, an acronym for Community Activities Rallying Everyone to Serve, was started under The President's Challenge. BB21 Programme initiative, chaired by Mr Khoo Boon Hui, was kicked off to review and improve the BB Programme so that we remain an attractive and effective youth organisation.

2002	BB Adventure Quest (BBAQ) was launched at Nanyang Technological University. BBAQ became an annual gruelling event where Boys go through various checkpoints to complete the given tasks over a 6 to 10 hours period.
2003	The first BB Pipes & Drums Festival, where Pipes & Drums bands from various Companies pitch their piping skills, was held at the Esplanade Park. BB began a long term project to establish the BB Learning Centre in Prayut Village, Cambodia. BB seeks to provide a structured BB programme that will help to develop the youths in Cambodia. Since its inception, the first Cross of Heroism was awarded to WO Jeffrey Jiang of 12(I) Singapore Company for his bravery in saving a man's life when on a community service project in Thailand.
2005	BB celebrates its 75th Anniversary. BB was honoured to have President S R Nathan host an Appreciation Dinner at the Istana for our volunteer officers. The inaugural President's Award Presentation Ceremony was held at the Istana, where the first batch of deserving recipients were presented the highest award in BB by President S R Nathan.
2006	The Boys' Brigade Learning Centre in Siem Reap, Cambodia was officially opened with close to 50 youth attending classes regularly. Goals and Strategies 2010 was formulated to propel the BB forward to be in tune with the changing educational landscape. Four key thrusts for Goals 2010 were identified: namely Strengthening Programmes; Officers, Relationships and Companies, On Strategies 2010, five focus areas were identified: namely Programmes Excellences, Systems and Processes, Clusters Resource, Communications Plan and Financial Plan.
2007	BBSGB celebrates its 20th anniversary. Cluster Consultations sessions were promulgated to develop and engage officers on the ground to collaborate resources within the BB family.

Sean Lai, 27th Singapore, who has worked tirelessly in promoting Planet BB around Singapore.

The Boys' Brigade 27th Singapore Company Story

National Day's parade in Li Sun High with Mr Pao (left) and Mr Edward Chan (right).

27th Singapore Company was formed on 27 December 1968 in Li Sun High School, the only Chinese speaking Company in the Boys' Brigade. The late Captain, Mr Pao Ung Hwa, together with Rev Noah Chen and another officer, Mr See Yen Pai, a teacher, started the Company.

As the English Language was the main problem it did not participate in certain Brigade activities. Officers from the 8th Singapore Company were seconded to the 27th Singapore Company. They were Mr Edward Chan Kwok Chuen (2nd Captain; 1980 – 2002), Mr Roland Chan Kwok Hong and Mr Bobby Loh.

The Company in 1974.

An NCO residential Training Camp was held at Birkhall Rd Primary School. A batch of 12 keen and capable NCOs were then chosen. These young leaders later contributed greatly towards the achievements of the Company.

In the 70s and 80s, the Company excelled in physical activities, Brigade competitions such as the BCFT Games, Battalion Festival of Games, Inter-Coy games. Most of the Championship trophies were in our bag!

By 1976 the Company was the first Company in Singapore that had a Lion Dance Troupe and won the Fok Tai Loy's Challenge Trophy for BCFT (basketball, carrom, football, table tennis) Games. In 1978, the most triumphant event in our history was the winning of the National and Brigade Colours. Our Company also won the Tan Teck Khim's Challenge Cup (National Drill Competition). This Challenge Cup was retained by our Company

Our Champion team in 1978.

for another year after another equally triumphant win with Best Commander from our Company. In fact we had captured the trophy of the National Footdrill Competition 5 times and there was even a little publicity in the local English/Chinese papers.

Ever since we participated in Footdrill Competition, we were among the Best at Brigade level often finishing in the top 3 in the country. And in 2001 the Company was 1st in both Footdrill Competition & Creative Drill Competition

Our days at Li Sun High School were memorable and we used to have combined activities with our sister organization, the **5th Company Girls' Brigade.**

These activities included Combined Enrolment Service, Gospel/Evangelical Camp, Retreat and gatherings.

In 1981, after a long and proud career with the 27th Singapore Company, Mr Pao Ung Hwa finally stepped down as Captain. With his retirement, Mr Chan Kwok Chuen was appointed as the next Company Captain. Mr Pao was officially appointed as the Hon. Captain of the Company.

1983 marked another milestone in the history of the 27th. We moved into the big and busy estate of Ang Mo Kio, forming our Company at Presbyterian High School with a total strength of 120. Being the Centenary Year (1883-1983) of the BB, that year was an exceptionally great year for all in The Boys' Brigade with an abundance of interesting and unforgettable activities. We also managed to establish a skeleton Bagpipe Band with the assistance from Singapore Girls' Pipers. In 1985 The Company's Bagpipe Band was formed. Even though it was formed only that year, it was able to give a public performance. In 1987 the Company embarked on its first overseas expedition to Mount Ophir in Johor, Malaysia. About 30 Boys and officers participated. During the trip, we visited Yong Peng High School, in Johor, for some fellowship with the students.

In 1993, we celebrated our Silver Jubilee with lot of activities; Night Tour, Night Cycling and many more.

2001 saw the Company form its Bagpipe Band with strong support from the school. From 1992 till 2003, we participated in the Goodwill Tournament. In this tournament, about 5 Companies came together for 3 days of sports/games. These include Soccer U15/U18, Volleyball, Bas-

ketball, Carom, Archery, Chess, Table-Tennis, X-Country, Swimming, Badminton and many more. In our 12 years of participation, we were the Champion for 10 years, keeping the Challenge Cup and Shield. Our last Goodwill Tournament was in 2003.

During 2003 Mr Gavin Ong Chee Seng (our 3rd captain), an old boy of Presbyterian High School, took over the captaincy from Mr Edward Chan. The Company celebrated its 35th anniversary, this time with more interesting activities. We went for a hike from McRichite reservoir to Bukit Timah, and we also went Night Cycling. In November, we went on an educational tour to Thailand, visiting four Thailand BB Companies.

Two teams participated in the Adventure Quest in 2004, out of which one team came in 6th out of 71 teams. Ana a team comprising of only Sec1 boys represented the Company in the National Bible Quiz and achieved a Silver Honour Roll for the first time.

In a collaboration with the 93rd Company, we held Precision Drill performances at Orchard, Jurong Point & Ngee Ann City for the opening and closing ceremonies for the BBSGB and other external organizations. Together with the other Uniformed Groups, we participated in the Outdoor Mass Display for the school's Official Opening Ceremony.

2005 saw our Company achieve the JM Fraser Award (Gold). We won the first ever PHS Inter-UG Games, was awarded the Mrs. Carolin Tan Challenge Shield, and dominated in Basketball, Netball and Floorball. Two teams participated in the National Bible Quiz, out of which, one team made it into the tie-breaker round to achieve our Company's first Gold Honour Roll.

We had our first ever Combined PD performance with the Girls' Brigade 5th Company of our school during the Enrolment & Dedication Service. At the Awards Presentation Ceremony, we performed a unique Precision Drill performance with an element of 'STOMP' as a special item. We were given the honour to perform for our Prime Minister, Mr. Lee Hsien Loong, at the "River Hong Bao" during Chinese New Year.

As part of the school's 40th Anniversary celebrations, there was a special combined UG Precision Drill Display that we took part in.

In 2006 the Company achieved JM Fraser Award (Gold). SGT Jeriel Tan Li Siang won the 2nd place in the Category A, Bass Drumming Solo, at the Pipes & Drums Festival. We achieved a Gold Honour Roll for the second time in the National Bible Quiz. Two teams participated in the

From left: SSG Sim Jiang Wei, SSG Quek Zheng jie, WO Sean Lai, SSG Gregory Tan, SSG Lewis Tan, SSG Fabian Ng, WO Sia Keqin, WO Hong Yong Chun, SSG Darren Lim, SSG Ng Jun Ning, WO Phillip Subrata.

Adventure Quest achieved a Bronze Honour Roll despite the race ending earlier due to bad weather. Once again, we earned the spot as the champions for the PHS Inter-UG Games and were allowed to keep the Mrs. Carolin Tan Challenge Shield for the second year.

Another Combined PD team was formed with the GB 5th Company that performed for the 'Razzmatazz 2006 and Beyond' concert at Toa Payoh HDB Hub and for the "SYF in the Heartlands" event at Bishan Junction 8.

We achieved a Silver Honour Roll at the Adventure Quest with the Boys Team completing the race. It was the first time that a Boys, Relay and Open Team represented our Company.

The first ever online Company blog, "27online" was created to enable better communication through visual-audio means to cater to the IT revolution in the younger generation.

The Company produced a record 11 Founder's Men for the first time in 2007 at a separate lunch ceremony for the awards presentation. Company received JM Fraser Award (Gold Honour Roll) for Excellence!

Company celebrated her 40th Anniversary with special events throughout the year. We managed to obtain a Gold Honour Roll in the Adventure Quest, BB Week, & Character Quest in 2008. Company received JM Fraser Award (Silver Honour Roll) for Excellence!

Edited from the History and partly written by Senior Cadet Lieutenant Sean Lai.

Scrapbook photos of the 39th Singapore Company

by How Kar Koh

AQ team. My 2nd BB adventure quest in the year 2008.

Me and my fellow BB NCOs named ourselves the Big 8 for this picture!

My last photo with the Scouts who are also inside the colour party contingent.

One of my juniors took a picture with the rest of the uniform group which are from our school.

A formal picture taken with the primers and officer after our March Camp 2009.

A dinner with my ex-CCA mates 2008.

A photo with my officer in charge and my team mates 2009.

A group photo after the Nation day parade ends in school.

A shot from the HQ, they took a picture of me and my team reporting to the booth in the morning at 3am! For the BB adventure quest 2009.

Shawn Saimun Ang **Kodrat** of Singapore asked on Facebook…

Hey to all BB members!
I was just wondering whether any of you guys are like me. BB changed my life for the better. Character wise I'm more open and stuff! Hope to hear from you people!

Heya BB members!
Don't know about y'all, but BB has changed my life. Last time I used to be one who could not socialize well with others and was very much to myself most of the time. But through the various activities of the Boys' Brigade 27th Singapore Company; I have become more open with people!
To God Be the Glory!!

Stephan Chee. 27th Singapore

Hello to my fellow BB members,
To be honest I don't know whether BB has changed my life because I joined the 22nd Birmingham Boys Brigade at the age of 5 and have been there ever since, I'm now nearly 16. I could say that if I hadn't joined the Boys Brigade I wud be on the streets causing trouble or even banged up. So all I can say is this, thank Sir William Smith for founding the Boys Brigade. Amen Brother

Dean Painter (22nd Birmingham Boys Brigade RULES) LOL

Hi BB members,
I come from BB Indonesia. I would like to share you about how BB change my life...
When I was in junior high school I almost can't pass to the second grade because of my mark in my report.... so my cousin say to me if I cannot pass then BB would kick me out... I don't want to be kicked out from BB then I start to learn n study, not go out anymore then I can pass my test with a good report... Thanks for God that used BB to change my life.

Chen Min

I think we can all say that BB has helped us in some way. An elderly officer (of the 86th Birmingham Coy) in his seventies once said to me, often men would stop him in the street and say things like "Hello Mr Cragg. Do you remember me? I was once in the BB, and I would like to thank you for teaching me from a young age how to be a good person". These people were not necessarily Christians in their adult life, but they never forgot what the BB taught them, and have become good citizens.

David Chant

Trip to BBLC Cambodia

Going to the Boys' Brigade Learning Centre in Cambodia was truly an eye-opening experience that will stay with me for a long time to come. Having just emerged from Pol Pot's regime, Cambodia is fairly undeveloped. The people there are fairly distrusting of each other, as a result of the killings that took place only a few decades ago.

The trip to BBLC was undertaken with various members of my BB Company, the 60th Singapore Company of Raffles Institution, as well as other classmates and acquaintances. We went there to teach them fun and interactive lessons, such as English and recorder lessons, and also built a stretch of road outside the school leading to the main road.

We were doing drill with the guys.

Initially, we had adopted the mindset of teachers going to Cambodia. We were under the impression that we were going there to impart knowledge to them; to let them experience something that they would otherwise not get an opportunity to experience. However, we ended up being the students in the trip, as they taught us many important lessons about life and about interacting with people.

One of the things that we learnt about in Cambodia was that nothing is fixed. Lesson plans we created ended up thrown away, for we learnt that what the Cambodian children wanted to learn was completely different from what we had planned. We had planned to teach them songs like "Edelweiss", but we ended up teaching them various other songs that they wanted to learn

Another of the activities that we had planned for the children there was Chinese lessons. Since they spoke in Khmer and we spoke in English, it was indeed challenging to teach them how to communicate in a new language. It was indeed very heartening that they were very enthusiastic towards the lessons, and they constantly asked us to teach them how to translate various lines from English to Chinese.

Much of the interaction with the children, however, came not from structured lessons but instead through the spontaneous games and lessons that arose from talking to them. I remember one of the days when the children were talking about doing drill. We decided to hold a mock drill lesson for them, and it was indeed interesting to see them trying to learn to turn and march together as a squad!

There are many important lessons that the children there have taught us. One of them is that we should treasure the simple things that we have. Compared to our comfortable lives in Singapore, the children there really do not have many material possessions. Yet, they manage to live a contented life, making use of whatever they can find to play and have fun. Indeed, it leaves us embarrassed to think that we live on the other end of the spectrum, demanding many material possessions and constantly complaining about how life could be better.

Eventually, though, parting had to come. Parting is always the hardest part, and this was no exception. One of the children came up to me and said goodbye in Chinese. It was really a mix of emotions. On one hand, we were sad to leave them, yet this sadness was being mitigated by the knowledge that they had managed to learn things during our visit.

After coming back from Cambodia, we go back to our lives, to the hustle and bustle of Singapore, and we leave behind the life experienced in Cambodia. However, the same cannot be said for the children over there. People like us, we come and go, but they will probably stay in that village for a long time to come. What we have brought for them comes not so much in tangible terms. After all, we only built a road for them in the time we were there. There are things that we can leave behind though. One of these are the lesson plans. 5 days is a very short span of time, and it is definitely not enough for them to learn as much as we would want them to learn. The onus is thus on them to carry the passion for learning in their hearts. Also, and more importantly, we have brought hope for the children.

Hope that one day when they grow up, they will be able to become useful citizens. Hope that they will be able to carve a proper life for themselves with skills that they have learnt. Hope that they will be able to make a difference. Most importantly, hope that they will love and trust each other.

Nathanael Foong, Senior Cadet Lieutenant
BB 60th Company Singapore
Raffles Institution

The Cambodian guys took us to see their village.

The BB in Brunei

Brunei Darussalam, which translates as **Brunei –The Abode of Peace**, aptly describes this small jewel country set in the North-West of the Island of Borneo, where forests cover 80% of the interior land with main towns located along its narrow coastal belt. It is a small rich **oil and natural gas** producing state.

The climate rarely varies from a humid 29° to 33° year round. Although Brunei Darussalam is outside the typhoon belt, rainfall is high, varying from 2500mm a year (100 inches) along the coastal belt to 5000mm a year (200 inches) in certain parts of the interior. Vegetation is lush and most of the country is covered by primary and secondary rain forest with only a narrow coastal strip of land being cultivated.

Brunei Darussalam became a fully independent member of the British Commonwealth on 1 JAN 1984 and is ruled by His Majesty Sultan Haji Hassanal Bolkiah. His Majesty is 29th in his family line going back to the 15th Century when Brunei was the centre of a powerful empire covering most of the northern part of the island of Borneo. The **population** of Brunei is 380,000.

The official **language** is Bahasa Melayu or the Malay language. English is widely spoken as well as several Chinese dialects. The official **religion** is Islam, with religious tolerance practiced towards non-Muslims.

The 1st Brunei BB Company was **started** on 19th JULY 1964 By Mr. Charlie Keasberry at the **Anglican Church** Mission St Andrew's, Bandar Seri Begawan, BRUNEI then known as Brunei Town. He first came to hear about the "Blue Boys" as far back as 1958 when he was in Penang for training. He was a dental technician, by profession, working with the Government Medical Centre. His impression about the "Blue Boys" was that of the bell boys who were working in the hotel service industry and attend to hotel customers when they check into the hotels.

Back home Mr. Charlie Keasberry enquired about the activities of the "Blue Boys" from friends from the Church in Penang. They provided him with the name and address of Mr. S.P. Chua of Singapore and advised him to write to Mr. S.P. Chua, who in return, sent Mr. Charlie some of the materials among one of the materials was on "How to start a BB Company".

Mr. Keasberry was a Scout leader during that time but relinquished his involvement in the Scout movement and subsequently became the 1st Captain of 1st Brunei. He was assisted by a Singaporean, Mr. Phillip Lim, who was working with an Architect firm as a quantity surveyor. Mr. Lim was an Officer with the BB in his home country when he left to work in Brunei. His experience helped spur the work of The Brigade onward.

1st Brunei BB Company begun activities with 59 Boys under the sponsorship of St Andrew's of which a year later registered the 1st Girls' Brigade Company. In 1967 the BB brought in a Bugle and Fife band. The Bugle and Fife band still provide music for march past during sporting events as well as many other functions organized by other private schools and business establishments. The Boys' Brigade in Brunei was the 1st and still the ONLY youth organization to have a Bugle and Fife Band of its own until today. There is no plan to change it. Many brass bands from especially government schools came and went but the BB Bugle and Fife band is still popular among the general public.

Mr. Charlie Keasberry retired as Captain in 1975 and became the honorary Adviser to both the BB and GB Companies. The Captaincy was then taken over by Mr. Joseph Chin.

A 2nd Brunei BB Company, known as 1st Seria BB Company, was established in 1978 at the oil town Seria; 140 kilometers away from Bandar Seri Begawan. The Company was sponsored by another Anglican Church St Margaret's under the Captaincy of Mr. Daniel Keasberry. They met every Saturday afternoon.

The BB now meets every Sunday afternoon 1.30-4.30pm and an hour of brushing up on the Band, finishing at 5.30-6pm. Our programmes run from January to November of each year, with the AGM in early December, before Christmas.

In the interim, our plan is to organize some joint activity with the BB in Miri, Sarawak. Where situation permits and if feasible we would like to encourage some of our Boys to join BB Singapore at their year-end annual camp.

Our **mission** is to assist Boys, develop their character and spiritual maturity with the use of CE materials such as the *Navigators* and *Walk thru the Bible* series. We also try to immerse the Boys into the Church as altar servers and choir members. Mentoring the Boys to love, care and help the needy in the community by helping out at the various centres.

On the Brigade Corporate front our **vision** over the next 5 years is to identify potential prospects for involvement of young working people as future **Leaders** of the organization. The Leadership role is still both honorary and voluntary. While this is a long term strategy we have been putting out extracts about our Leadership need in the Church Bulletin on a regular basis beginning 2008. In the meantime, we request assistants from former Boys and Officers, when we organize major events such as the annual camp and other outdoor activities.

Our goal "Character Building and Good Discipline" remains central in the Organisation. Character building is based on the example of Biblical Christian characters both in the Old and New Testament. This has been emphasized over the past many years in the CE Curriculum. There is no intention to change this goal in the foreseeable future.

The local BB Theme has been "The Boys' Brigade Brunei – Where Good Discipline Begins" It had generated positive acceptance among parents and resulted in the maintenance of the number in our BB membership when the theme was introduced since 1974. This is central in decision making for many parents and guardians who entrusted their children to us.

Very limited extension works are truly being undertaken by The Brigade in Brunei. We are still 1 Company and our strategy is confined to expanding our number within this unique Company alone.

We have a Church in Cebu City, Philippines which has requested us to help them start a BB Company there. We have entered into discussion with their Church Board and have agreed, in principle, to look further into the issue. The Boys will not wear uniform but just simply a BB T-shirt. The Church will look for a full time seminary trained youth worker, for which BB Brunei will pay a USD50.- monthly subsistence stipend. The establishment of the BB Company has not been realized yet and needed more concrete final discussions.

Membership is open to all Boys who wish to join us. They join us at the age of 7 years old. We do not limit the religious belief of these Boys and accept them as member regardless of their faith. As such we have member who are either Hindu, Buddhist or free thinkers, among our Protestant or Roman Catholic Boys.

We not only accept into membership Boys from the Anglican Church School but also Boys who attend other Schools. Our members therefore comprises of Chinese, Indian, Thai, Filipinos, Indigenous and European Boys who join us from International, Government, Mission and private schools in the Brunei and Muara District. All the other 3 districts are not exposed to Brigade work. Interest to establish a Company in the Catholic School and another Christian Centre have been pursued but not followed through because new Christian based organizations cannot be legally registered due to the religious sensitivity in the country.

BB membership has been hovering around the 45-60 number brackets. The final membership number for 2008 is 46 inclusive of 3 Officers.

A regular community project is the co-operative "Gotong Royong" work for the Old Person's Home and inmates for the "mentally and physically challenged" institutions. There are at least 4 such private institutions which conduct regular sales of handiwork made by inmates. As part of their community badge our Boys work in these institutions, by arrangements, for 20 hours.

Children in Brunei juggle around school, extra tuition classes, swimming/piano/music lessons, sports, martial art and a myriad of other pursuits. Despite all these busy schedules, life style in Brunei is still that of comfort. Boys choose to **participate** in activities which suit their comfort and liking. Outdoor activities under the hot sun attract less than 20 Boys. Indoor activities, without question of course, bring out the whole Company. Picnic is therefore rarely organized.

We foresee future growth in recruitment in the country as promising. With obesity rampant among 1 in every 3 children in the nation, the Ministry of Health in collaboration with the Ministry of Education have made it compulsory for every school children to take up one uniform group, among 2 other activities, as part of their extra curriculum participation.

Edited version of a report prepared by Mr. Walter YEE
BRUNEI 22 SEPT 2008

The history of the BB in Indonesia

This is the history of The Boys' Brigade in Indonesia. The original article was from Indonesian Wikipedia (written by Lt. Karnadi Lim, a friend of mine), and this translation was done for a BB member from Hong Kong who was in contact with me as part of her International badge last year (2008).

There was an idea to extend The Boys' Brigade to Indonesia somewhere in the sixties. It was only in 1984, however, that Mr. Sam Tan paid a visit to Medan at the invitation of the Methodist Church of Indonesia, who later sent a few requests to Singapore to know more about the Boys' Brigade's operations and their ministry in the church. In June 1984, Pastor PH Pasaribu, Pastor RPM Tambunan and Pastor J Gultom went to Singapore to learn about The Boys' Brigade under Mr. Lim Khay Tham of Singapore. This was followed by more visits between Medan and Singapore, and vice-versa.

As a result of the training by BB Singapore, the first BB Indonesia Company, 1st Medan Selatan was set up. This was followed by 2nd Mandala Company, and later 3rd East Medan Company.

With its first Company set up in 1986, the Boys' Brigade Indonesia employed an Executive Secretary to administer the Boys' Brigade activities. And the first president of BB Indonesia was Pastor PH Pasaribu.

The assistance provided by BB Singapore was not only limited to visitations, but even material assistance was given to BB Indonesia as a backbone for their operations.

The next visit was carried out by the Captain of 40th Singapore Company, Mr. Richard Tan, in which he followed up where Mr. Lim Khay Tham had left off earlier. In his visits, he expressed desire for The Boys' Brigade Indonesia to expand beyond Medan.

Our BB Drill Camp at Jakarta district.

BB Indonesia Camp Bersama 2005.

After the formation of the 1st Medan Selatan Company, the BB had a decline in activities for a period of time, and all the Companies formed were inactive. In June 1991, the Central Methodist Administration sent 4 representatives which consisted of Mr. Horbanus Simanjuntak, Mr. Petrus CF, Madam Resien and Madam Meisien. They were sent for training to revive the BB Indonesia.

After returning from Singapore, Horbanus Simanjuntak was appointed the Executive Secretary, working at the Methodist Church of Indonesia Central Administration, at Hang Tuah Road No.8, Medan. The Administrative work was carried out by the Executive Secretary. At that time, two new Companies were active, which was the 4th Markoni Company, and 5th Tanjung Morawa Company.

A simple uniform was first worn on the 22nd of November 1991, by the 5th Tanjung Morawa Company, and later more uniform accessories were gradually added on. In December 1991, the Boys' Brigade celebrated their first "Natal Bersama" (Christmas Together) celebration at the Methodist Church of Indonesia, Markoni.

The Boys' Brigade Indonesia became a member of the World Conference in 1992, which meant an automatic membership in the East Asia Regional Fellowship (EARF), which is part of World Conference. Mr. Eric Woodburn visited The Boys' Brigade in Medan, Indonesia.

With limited knowledge about camping, The Boys' Brigade had their first camp in 1992, at Lawang Hill. The objective of this camp was to encourage fellowship among the Companies which were active. And it has now become an annual event which is organized by The Boys' Brigade headquarters.

In 1992, for the first time, future officers of Companies that were going to be formed were given the opportunity to follow a basic training in Kampar, Malaysia. Among the candidates sent for the training was Balal Simorangkir (Methodist Church of Indonesia, Mandala), Budi Pasaribu (M.C. of I, Reinata), Meishe (M.C. of I, Lubuk Pakam,) and July (M.C. of I, Perbaungan). All four of the candidates were accompanied by the Executive Secretary, Mr. Petrus and a Senior Officer, Reisien.

1993 was the first time The Boys' Brigade in Indonesia had a friendly competition amongst the Companies, which is held annually every July.

Chiew Kin-yan Darryn

Chen Min from Indonesia sent the following email about his Company

Hi.... My name is Danny Tandela from 1st Bandung Company. They call me Mr Danny, but I am known as Chen Min.

I join the Boys' Brigade since I was 13 years old, now I am 21. It means that I had been in BB for 8 years (I was in the 12th Medan, a big company with 120 member for a year).

Well BBI is separate in 2 island. Java and Sumatera. BBI was started from Sumatera Island. Sumatera has about 6 active company as I know and in Java island is separate to big city like Jakarta, Bandung, Semarang and Surabaya. The biggest one is in Jakarta about 8 company. There are over 2300 member in BBI. Well next year 2011 BBI will celebrate 25th years. But we are still on our progression. As u know BB can be church-based and school-based. Well in Sumatera Island BB is under Methodist church because all the active company is a Methodist school. In Java almost all of the company is school-based.

Left to right: Beata Megan, Chen Min and Patty Si Pej ho.

I used to travel by bus to help at BB... almost 2 hour by road. I am drill instructor... last time 1-3 May BB Jakarta make the first Drill Camp, n I the trainer. Hehehehe...

Right: Chen Min.

Please pray for us as BB grow in Indonesia.

The BB in Indonesia was founded in 1986. Mr Lim Khay Tham train up Petrus C.F. (now is the BB vice president in Indonesia).

Now I am taking my industrial engineering university at bandung in java island. You still understand? Sorry if I have a bad English. Wakakakakaka.

BB Asia Climb 2009

We gathered from March 21 to 24, 2009 for BB Asia's Mount Kinabalu Climb, to raise funds for BB Indonesia, Thailand, Philippines and Cambodia – a tradition initiated by Paul "Robokop" Juby in 1999. Paul, age 78, with two artificial hips, had trained hard for this, his fourth and last climb.

Stephen Liew, our attentive host, warmly welcomed us to a hearty fellowship dinner at Kinabalu Park. Paul noted: "this is *more* than just about raising funds – we are a fellowship of friends from U.K., Hong Kong, Malaysia and Singapore – to encourage our fellow Brigaders around Asia." It had all started with a challenge ten years ago from Paul's former BB Boy, Michael Moorthy – now BB Malaysia and BB Asia President. Michael spoke of BB Asia's pioneering work and how BB Malaysia's Girls' Wing now produces a steady crop of lady officers. For me, I was especially happy to have my wife Carol (ex-Girls' Brigade) join in the climb.

Next day came the challenge: a mountain to climb! After breakfast and worship, Michael flagged us off, with Robokop leading the way. We had a sunny start, and were soon blessed with drizzles, light and heavy rain – our wettest climb so far! BB Hong Kong's team of mountaineering Auxiliaries accompanied Paul all the way to Gunting Lagadan hostel. Said a very tired but happy Paul: "I sang *Walking with Jesus* along the way!" After dinner we retired to rest for the evening.

We assembled at 3 a.m., forming two teams: Team 1 aimed to reach the summit for sunrise, while Team 2 accompanied Paul. After a prayer, we set off into the cold, pitch dark. Our guide

Michael Moorthy and Paul 'Robokop' Juby.

led the way and our headlamps lit our path. Step by careful step, we negotiated the upward trails; altitude effects; and challenging rope climbs up and round a steep bend. Eventually, I slowed down to a crawl and fell behind my team. I observed a father comforting his son, who was bent over, overcome by altitude sickness. Said father to son: "It's ok, we can turn back and go down, son." I sat down too, to rest my pounding heart and catch my breath. As the crescent moon sank, dawn broke. Early morning light lifted my spirits. I remembered that the Brigade flag was in my satchel! My team members must be anxiously waiting for me at the summit. With renewed strength, I continued slowly up the seemingly unending uphill plain, taking very small steps – a very long journey. Then came the last hurdle: an exhausting crawl up rocks and boulders to the summit at Low's peak – 4,095 M above sea level. I was overjoyed to meet my team members. We unfurled our BB flag at the summit. *Lord, we ask Thy blessings, on The Boys' Brigade!*

Below the wind and above the clouds, we admired panoramic views of the mountain peaks and valleys of beautiful Sabah. After this exhilarating experience, we made our way down to Gunting Lagadan for sumptuous meals, wonderful naps, great fellowship and sweet sleep.

Next day, we began our journey down. I was in awe of clouds gently rolling into the serene mountain forest and admired some pitcher plants. Paul remarked: "God said to me: 'don't forget to thank Me when you get down!'" And he did, after a very carefully guided and exhausting effort, with the expert help of the local guides, Stephen and Lois (on her 30th climb!). Well done Robokop!

Back at Kota Kinabalu, we celebrated with a thanksgiving dinner. Our Chaplain, Rev. Richard Tok reflected: "This climb is like our journey of faith. We meet problems along the way. We need encouragement and help. When I looked up at the many little head lamps

winding up to the summit, it looked so far away I wondered if I would make it down alive! But thanks to support from my teammates, I made it to the summit and back!" Jokes and fond memories were shared between Paul and Michael – a friendship which began as BB Officer and Boy some forty years ago!

We had each persevered to reach for our goals. And then, we said our goodbyes – until we meet again, God willing – to challenge this magnificent mountain. Thank you, Robokop, for showing us that with God's help, nothing is impossible if we persist to scale the heights!

Pang Seng Hock. Thursday, April 09, 2009

The BB 38th Hong Kong

The Boys' Brigade, Hong Kong, was founded in 1959. Till now, there are over 200 Companies and over 5000 members who belong to different churches, youth centres, and schools in different districts.

Our Company was founded in 1985 by Shatin Methodist Church. We have gathering from 2:30pm to 5:15pm every Saturday in Shatin Methodist Collage. All members must wear tidy uniform. Normally gathering consists of fellowship, drill and professional skill training such as camping, first aid, and sports; training will have badges awarded to qualified members. Members with good performance will be appointed to be NCO (Non-Commissioned Officer), and receive NCO leader training.

We welcome boys and girls who are over 8 years old to apply to be members. If you are Christian, over 18 years old (Male or Female), and would like to devote your life to train young people, you are recommended to apply to be one of us.

We have a chaplain and a captain. Besides, we have 2 lieutenants and 4 warrant officers. Moreover, we have 5 NCOs.

Currently, our Company has 12 Company section members and 12 junior section members, which consist of both boys and girls.

Language Used: Mostly Chinese (Speaking in Cantonese).

Daniel Edmond So

The author recently received a fantastic new book, from Priscilla Lee BBHK 40th Company, covering the 50th Anniversary of BBHK.

Borneo, Malaysia – Sibu & Kuching in the State of Sarawak

The Founder – Sarawak

In 1958, Mr. Charles Henry Ingka, aged 25 returned home from Singapore after having been there since 1947. In 1948, while studying in St. Andrew's School, he had joined the BB. Later he became an Officer. Mr. Ingka saw the need for proper training among Kuching Boys and he knew that BB was the answer. With the support of Provost Anthony Perry, Mr. Ingka set out to lay the foundations for Brigade work in Kuching. He came back with nothing of BB except that which was in his heart and mind. He had never expected to start BB in Kuching, or anywhere in Sarawak, but he did in early 1961. The 1st Kuching Company, the first Boys' Brigade Company on the island of Borneo was established and marched into the pages of history. Since then, BB grows steadily across the Land of the Hornbill.

Today, BB Sarawak has the most number of BB Companies in Malaysia with a total membership of more than 3,000 Members. The 32 Companies are spread across the major towns of the Sarawak (Kuching-9 Companies; Sri Aman-1 Company; Sarikei-2 Companies; Bintangor-1 Company; Sibu-10 Companies; Mukah-1 Company; Bintulu-2 Companies; Miri-5 Companies; Limbang-1 Company). There are 2 Companies (9th Sibu & 9th Kuching) sponsored by a local church denomination, SIB (Sidang Injil Borneo, the localized name for Borneo Evangelical Mission, BEM) and 1st Sibu has the biggest membership of more than 500 strong.

BB Company helping with work on the Christian Children's Centre, Uganda.

BB Company at Namirembe St. Paul's Cathedral, Kampala, Uganda.

Wisconsin, USA. Rifle range shooting practice.

1st Thailand Company parade.

Tim Rogers from Australia (centre) visits Thailand and Cambodia, here with Lawrence Tay and Tony Chew.

6th Thailand Bible Study class.

BB in Brunei.

Ganaway Activity Centre, Millisle, Northern Ireland.

8J Singapore Company, helping out in a local Primary School.

1st Johor Bahru Company, All-girls drill team in Malaysia.

Beating Retreat Ceremony and Presentation of Queen's Men, UK.

Beating Retreat Ceremony and Presentation of Queen's Men, UK.

BB in Indonesia.

1st Sibu-Malaysia's biggest Company.

Community Works

Raise funds for National Kidney Foundation (NKF). In 2008, we manage to hand-over 2 units of Dialysis Machines for NKF, Kuching branch.

Love-In-A-Box Project (LIAB) – collect gifts for the unfortunate/poor people during Christmas season.

Other Programmes

Every Company will hold annual evangelistic rally for the members.
State Events (Advanced NCOs Training Course, State Camp).
Regional (Basic NCOs Training Course, Competitions, Games, Camps, joint programmes).

The Unreached Area

Extension has always been the main focus of BB Sarawak to uphold BB Object, the advancement of Christ's Kingdom. We pray to extend BB to many more promise land and set BB flag on high. With Christ as our Greatest Captain, march the Mighty Band of Brothers, on the land of the Hornbill.

Thanks to **Wei Ung** for supplying this article written by **Sarawak State Commissioner, Honorary Captain Lo Hoi Fook**.

Drill.

50th Anniversary International Camp

International camp is the grand event for The Boys' Brigade in Hong Kong held every 5 years. In late December 2009 we welcomed 235 guests from 6 countries or regions including Australia, Thailand, Malaysia, Indonesia, Singapore and Macau, to celebrate with us our 50th anniversary, and join our 50th Anniversary International camp.

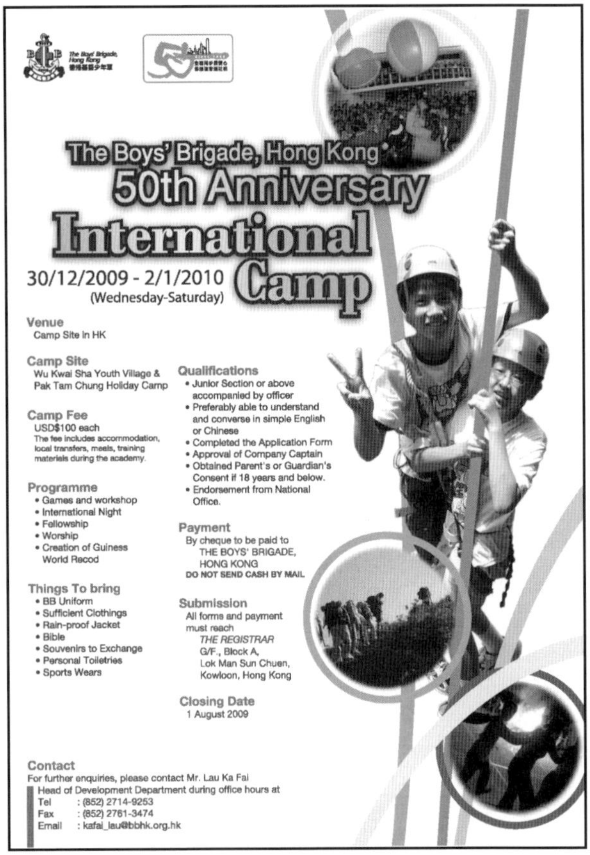

Most of the overseas campers came to Hong Kong a few days earlier or stayed behind after the camp, so the headquarters of BBHK organized a group of HK Officers and Brigaders to act as ambassadors. I am one of the ambassadors serving the Officers and Brigaders from 1st Sibu Company in Malaysia.

1st Sibu came 4 days before the camp and my friends and I led them around Hong Kong. We tried different means of transport in Hong Kong, such as MTR, buses, mini buses, trams, Peak tram, and Star ferry. We had also sampled various kinds of food in Hong Kong, including Dim Sum, Wanton noodles, Canton-style congee and milk tea. We visited the Peak on the coldest day of the winter!

In the camp, together with other Hong Kong and overseas campers, we counted down 2010 and we tried to break the Guinness record by making the longest (>800m) paper doll chain in the world. We had lots of fun in Hong Kong and some of the overseas campers said they will come and join our 2014 International Camp.

You missed the chance? You wanna come and join us and have some fun? Put down 2014 BBHK International Camp in your schedule right now!

W/O Priscilla Lee, 40th Company of BBHK

The BB in Thailand

How The Boys' Brigade came to be in Thailand

The Boys' Brigade Ministry has come to Thailand by cooperation between The Boys' Brigade Malaysia and The Boys' Brigade in Singapore. In December, 1993 Mr. Michael Moorthy, The President of Boys' Brigade in Malaysia and the Girls' Brigade in Singapore came to Thailand to introduce the Boys' Brigade ministry to some pastors and some School administrations and then brought some of them to visit Singapore and Malaysia for BB & GB ministry observation. Later on in 1994 two BB Companies were established in Bangkok.

The 1st BB Thailand Company belongs to Thai Christian School, Bangkok by Mr. Prasert Pornkeeratikool and Mr. Chumnan Pattakittikoon.

The 2nd BB Thailand Company belongs to Jai Samarn Church, Bangkok.

Later on, other Companies were formed in 1995, these are:

3rd Company belong to Mahachai Christian Vittaya School, Samutsakorn Province,
4th Company belong to Konkaen Christian School, Konkaen Province,
5th Company belong to Christhum Vittaya Christian School, Bangkok,
6th Company belong to Hua Kun-jae Christian School, Chonburi Province,
7th Company belong to Hua Kun-jae Church, Chonburi Province,

As of today (2009) we have 22 BB Companies in Thailand.

From Left: Mr Ho Meng Wai (BB Singapore) Mr Prasert Pornkeeratikul (President of BB Thailand), Mr Paul Juby & his wife (BB UK), Anna Glinhom (Wells) (1st fulltime staff of BB Thailand), Mr Roland Chan (BB Singapore), Mr Micheal Moorthy & his wife Janet President of BB Malaysia & Founder of BB Thailand) This picture was taken in February, 1997, Bangkok.

I was a full time staff of Boys' Brigade Thailand since the beginning. Here are some photographs I would like to send to you. I am sorry that I cannot put a writing with the photos. so I would write them here to explain the photos. I hope you don't mind.
Any question please get back to me.

God bless you.

Anna Wells,

Thailand NCO's Training. At Mahachai Christian School, 1998.

The Boys' Brigade and The Girls' Brigade Officers Commissioner. At Hua Kunjae Church, Chonburi Province. 1996.

1st BB Thailand Company Camp. At Thai Christian School, Bangkok. January 21, 1995.

1st BB Thailand Company Award Ceremony. Thai Christian School, 1995 (Full Uniform for the beginning of BB in Thailand).

1st BB Thailand Company Award Ceremony. Thai Christian School, 1995. Praise the Lord with Special Song.

Drill Section with half uniform. At 1st Thailand BB Company, 1995.

Tim's amazing trip!

My name is Tim Rogers and I am a BB Officer in Australia. I joined BB when I was seven years old as have been in BB for 15 years now. From April-June of 2009, I had the opportunity to visit Thailand and observe how BB was operating.

The Boys' Brigade in Thailand was started in 1994 as an initiative of the Boys' Brigade Asia community. Currently there are 12 active Companies and over 1200 members. Both The Boys' Brigade and The Girls' Brigade operate in Thailand. Some Companies operate alongside a Girls' Brigade Company at the same location while others choose to run a co-educational program under the leadership structure of either BB or GB.

10th Thai group.

Since BB was first introduced to Thailand, over 25 Companies have been founded in schools and Churches all over the country. Some Churches have decided to suspend BB in favour of programs designed to reach poorer communities and their families. These churches are generally keen to restart BB in the future when and if circumstances are favourable and leadership personnel become available. BB is currently investigating how it can participate alongside these ministries, and even begin work into "slum" areas of Bangkok and other cities.

The Boys' and Girls' Brigades in Thailand is also run as part of the curriculum in some Christian Schools around the country. Conducting BB and GB in schools gives students the opportunity to play games, sing songs and learn Bible verses. Most students are not from Christian families and, if not for BB and GB, would not have any another opportunity to take part in Christian teaching in a mode that is relevant for their age group.

1st Thailand Company cooking.

During my time in Thailand, I visited Churches and schools operating BB, and was able to witness the tremendous ministries operating in local communities. For many of the youth in these communities, BB is their only contact with Church. These ministries are clearly striving towards fulfilling the Object of the Boys' Brigade in Thailand: namely "The advancement of Christ's Kingdom among members ... " I also had the opportunity to talk with representatives from Churches who wish to start BB in their communities as a way of reaching out to the local young people.

I had the chance to visit BB Companies in and around Bangkok, as well as regional administrative centres including Khon Kaen, Chonburi and Nakhon Ratchasima. As well as encourage the local BB Officers and members, I was able to share a little bit about BB in Australia and show pictures of the differences in our uniforms. In the future I hope to organize more trips for BB and GB members in Australia as a way of opening their eyes to Global ministry.

Upon arriving in Thailand, I was greeted at the airport by two representatives of BB Thailand, including the newest member of the BB staff, Tum, who is now serving the Lord at the BB headquarters in Klang Toey, south-west Bangkok. After a night spent in a hotel, we were off to the city of Kanchanaburi to stay at a Church that previously ran a Boys' Brigade program, but has since decided that a Compassion program would be more appropriate for the kids living in the slum area where the Church is situated. While in Kanchanaburi, I had the chance to visit Allied War cemeteries, the Bridge over the river Kwai, and attended the annual dawn service commemorating Australia POW's who died while constructing the Thailand-Burma railway during World War II.

After heading back to Bangkok, we proceeded to the Rangsit Methodist Church, about 1 hour north of Bangkok. The Pastor of this church is the Reverend Prasert Pornkiratikul and is the current President of BB in Thailand. I stayed at the Church for a week and participated in the Church's annual "Cross camp," teaching English, as well as making relationships with the campers. The Camp finished on the Friday and the BB Company (10th Thailand) held its first meeting for the year, the following day. I was able to share games and even teach figure marching to the BB members, which was thoroughly enjoyed by both the members and Officers.

After returning from Rangsit, I had the opportunity to visit the Northern city of Chiang Mai to visit some family friends who are running a children's home. I had the chance to talk with several people about BB as a ministry, and make a few contacts on behalf of BB Thailand. After a week in Chiang Mai, I headed north to the city of Khon Kaen and its only Christian School, where Boys' and Girls Brigade is part of the curriculum (4th and 5th Thailand respectively). The Principal of the school is Mrs Songsri Tangtragulpaisan, who is the Vice-president of BB Thailand. She is very active in promoting BB in Thailand to her many friends and associates in Thailand's Christian Community. While staying at the school, I helped to teach English classes for students ranging from upper primary to senior middle school. I also had the chance to share a little about BB in Australia and teach some Australian games. I

Me and my dad at Tonle Sap river, Cambodia.

With Singapore mission team and students at BB learning centre, Siem Reap.

Me at Royal Palace Cambodia.

stayed in Khon Kaen for two weeks and it was great to get to know students and encourage them in their studies and Christian lives. I also had the chance to visit a few of the region's tourist attractions including the Cobra village and some local churches in the area.

While staying in Khon Kaen, I also had the chance to visit the 23rd Thailand Company in the city of Nakhon Ratchashima. This Church was very proud of its small (about 25 members), yet vibrant BB ministry and were reporting a sizable growth in members from previous years. While in Nakhon Ratchashima, I accompanied Principal Songsri and other BB representatives from the school, to visit a church which is keen to start a BB program. This church already organizes English classes on a Saturday morning with a sizable attendance. They are interested in starting BB as a program that can assist the Church to reach out to the local youth.

I then headed back to Bangkok, then to a city about 1 hour west of Bangkok to visit Mahachai Christian School. I had the opportunity to share about Australia with the students and attend the BB Company (3rd Thailand). While in Mahachai, I had the opportunity to visit the famous floating markets, ride in a long tail boat and try some of the famous Mahachai seafood. I also had the chance to stay for church at the Mahachai Baptist Church from which the school was founded.

The following day I travelled back to Bangkok then to the Chon Buri province about 2 hours east of Bangkok. I stayed at the Hua Koonchae Christian School and taught a few English lessons to the middle school. On the Wednesday I participated in the BB program (2nd Thailand) and shared with the seniors about BB Australia before playing a few games with them. After BB, I headed straight back to Bangkok to visit the 1st Thailand Company at Thailand Christian College on Thursday and Friday. We sang songs, played games and I shared about BB in Australia and I answered a lot of questions! On Saturday I stayed in Bangkok, to visit the 23rd Thailand Company at a Church in a suburb called Klong Toey. After sharing with the boys and girls, we played games, and then after BB I got to see the Church's football ministry located on the 5th (top) floor of the Church! It was great to see.

On Sunday I went back to Chon Buri to visit the 6th Thailand BB Company that operates at the Hua Koonchae Church. Both the 6th and 2nd Thailand Companies meet at the same location but on different days (Wednesday and Sunday). They share some members and most officers. Some boys who had graduated from middle school (and therefore now attend another school) still come to 6th Company so they can continue to attend BB.

On Monday I headed back to Bangkok again to visit BB at the Bangkok Christian College (15th Thailand). This school is the oldest and one of the largest private schools in Thailand. The BB is run by a dedicated team of Chaplains who organize BB for grades 4, 5 and 6 during lunch break on Monday, Tuesday and Wednesday respectively. The Officers hope that in the future they might have enough staff to expand the BB ministry into middle and seniors school grades.

The following weekend, I met my dad in Bangkok and we flew to Cambodia. We visited many places in Phnom Penh including "The Killing Fields", the Royal Palace, and eat dinner on the banks of the Mekong River. While in Phnom Penh we also had the chance to visit World Vision, and see my sponsor child Den, whom I have sponsored for around 7 years. We then took the bus to Siem Reap to see Angkor Wat, the largest temple complex in the world.

2nd Thailand Company parade.

While in Siem Reap we visited the Boys Brigade Learning Centre. We had a chance to meet with the staff of one of the regular mission teams from BB Singapore who visit. We then had the chance to sit in on one of the centre's daily English classes, which it provides free of charge to local students. That afternoon we flew back to Phnom Penh and the next day we flew back to Bangkok.

I stayed one more night in Bangkok, then started my journey back to Australia. I had a 24 hour stopover in Kuala Lumpur Malaysia during which I had the chance to visit the 3rd Kuala Lumpur Company at the YMCA. I got to experience a bit of BB Malaysian style, which means I loved every minute of it. I was really encouraged by the attitude of the boys and their dedication to the Company. They did themselves proud. The next morning I flew back to Australia arriving home in the evening to be greeted by friends and family.

What a trip! Every step of the journey was blessed and I will never forget the great experiences and the wonderful people that I met. I would encourage anyone who is keen to do a similar trip and visit BB in their area of the globe. You will be an amazing encouragement to the people you meet and learn a great deal from the experience. God Bless.

A Shoestring Journey of a Brigadier around Europe...

When I was still with The Boys' Brigade, 1st Sarikei Company back in the 1990s, I often heard some parents complain about the amount of time their son spent in BB activities (band, drill, camping etc). Some even sarcastically pointed out that you can't go far, or it is useless to spend lots of time in BB and tried to mock us. Now I can prove to you; **YES** you can go very far with the things that you learnt in The Boys' Brigade. I finished my bachelor degree locally and landed myself as a scholar of a very prestigious scholarship from European Union to study multidisciplinary engineering field in Paris (France), Madrid (Spain) and Stockholm (Sweden). Counting gracefully, I have been living and travelling a lot in Europe for the past 3 years.

From the perspective of a Brigadier...

Between two worlds, Europe and South East Asia.... There are huge differences in language, culture, lifestyle, time, distance, food, weather; just to name a few. Yes, there is a huge barrier to overcome BUT, isn't that the interesting part of life? To me, the answer is definitely YES; packed with all the knowledge (courses/awards) and skills that I learnt in 16 years as a member, NCO and Officer of The Boys' Brigade. After all, integration, adaptation, planning, socializing skills require courage, communication, wisdom and reverence to do so. And, I learnt those soft skills in The Boys' Brigade. I salute to all present and previous Officers of the Boys' Brigade in Malaysia, 1st Sarikei Company. Thanks to my parents for being so supportive and constructive. You guys did a wonderful job in equipping and teaching me.

Europe in general provides a huge platform for discovery, culture and language exchanges, travel, beautiful and yet diverse landscapes. Modern Western Europe is the birthplace of Western culture and the birth of modern society. The Alps form the remarkable piece of nature which borders several countries and cultures. On the west, the English Channel has a fantastic masterpiece of engineering work; high speed train system under the sea. The merging of the wild, medieval and modern Europe assimilated so well that it remains a priceless yet very attractive place to be discovered.

A single step to mark the beginning...

Paris is a world class city to live in; coined as the lovers' city which is true to certain extent. At the first sight, Paris is a relatively old medieval city but full with arts, music, unique street performers, magnificent architecture and not to mention the already popular list of tourist places such as *Notre Dame,* and *Tour Eiffel* in the guide book. Strolling along the Seine River in the day or at night reviews the elegant yet beautiful views of Paris; away from the hustle and bustle of the city. A day trip to *Château de Versailles* will definitely be fun and enjoyable especially in summer where you can visit the big English Garden behind the castle. In France, it is easier if you can speak French as most of people in the street don't speak English very well besides custom-made English for business. Public transportation is quite connected but always late or on strike or *La grève*. It is inside their blood and every now and then, you will hear it on the newspaper or TV. French cuisine and food is of the top notch in Europe and of course, it is quite pricey. French wine and cheese is fabulous as well; not forgetting the champagne and crepe!!

Going around France is relatively easy via train. A visit to *Chamonix, Mont Blanc* and surrounding area (*Annecy, Evian*) is a must for a nature or ski lovers. For catching the birds eye view of Mont Blanc, a helicopter ride is recommended. What a panoramic and magnificent view it is!! The gigantic glacier on the mountain slope, nice and fresh breeze slapping gently on your face, colourful leaves falling into the lake in autumn. One word to describe them all, magnificent. Going to the west of Paris you will reach another remarkable place, *Le Mont-Saint-Michel* which is an abbey situated on the rocky tidal island in Normandy commune. Here, you have to observe the high tide, it comes in very fast just like the horse running to the shore. There is a French saying "*La marée marche comme le cheval*". Summer is always a nice time to visit *Aix-en-provence, Côte d'Azur* and Mediterranean coastal area in south of France. As for castle lovers, a cycling trip in Blois along the Loire River is a must in summer or autumn. Christmas market in Strasbourg, Alsace is a good place to spend on Christmas gifts during winter. To all wine lovers who like to visit vineyards and wine tasting, Bordeaux is definitely the place you have to go.

55 minutes from Paris-*Gare du Nord* by TGV, you will reach the capital of Belgium, Brussels; passing through Mons and Wallonia regions. Belgian chocolate and wine are famous and well known, so a visit to chocolate museum and a bar is a must. A walk in Grand Place (market place) in summer will bring you to a spectacular display of colourful fresh flowers arranged on the ground. Since the EU administrative/parliament is here, a seat in the parliament sitting (10am) was another brand new experience for me.

A fast track train (Eurostar) will take you from here to St. Pancras Station which is in London, or you can fly directly from Paris Orly airport to London Luton/Stansted airport. The trip will take around an hour. Thames River, the London Eye, Big Ben, Tower Bridge, china town, guard changing at Buckingham Palace, Windsor Castle, Stonehenge, Bath, etc are not to be missed while you are there. An hour by flight from here, you will reach Edinburgh, Scotland. A trip to the highlands around Aberdeen, Glasgow, St. Andrew's and Edinburgh is highly recommended. Either way, a boat trip to Loch Ness or fresh water fishing trip is another option. Be cautious with the weather, quite wet and rainy in spring and summer. Glasgow, the place where The Boys' Brigade was founded is another milestone of my travels. I always wanted to visit this place to see the bagpipe, bugle, tartan etc. The city itself is relatively big but nothing much is here. It is like a sleeping town to me.

An hour and half back to mainland Europe will take you to Netherlands, the land under the sea level. Windmills are quite attractive to some, but lilies in Keukenhof garden are one of the best attractions in Holland. How about Dutch food? Milk forms a large portion of the Dutch diet. Dutch people have soup, milk and sandwich for lunch. Dinner is typically quite European and Italian. A visit to Venice is a must if you are in Europe but beware of the landmarks as you can easily get lost inside the maze of canals. Berlin, Germany provides a glimpse on the Berlin Wall, the contrast between East and West Germany and the reconstructed buildings after War World II. This quite cheap land is the largest country in the EU yet full of modern and high tech industries. The Bavarian region has nice beers and foods (knuckle of roasted pork with sour cabbage). There is an interesting castle; Neuschwanstein Castle or fairy tales castle which was the inspiration for sleeping beauty in Disneyland. A visit there is a must.

Thomas Moh.

Madrid, Spain, the land of 101 tapas and good food. Daily trips to small towns like Alvila, Cuenca, Toledo, Sevilla, Segovia and Salamanca is really an eye opener. Each of them is a small town with tall and high walls surrounding it and governed differently than each other. Sagrada familia, Montserrat, Olympic Park and Gothic museums in Barcelona are really interesting places to visit if you are a tourist. Afternoon siesta is observed strongly in Madrid and some cities in Andalusia; typical hot places but not throughout Spain. Ibiza, Valencia and Gran Canarias are famous for their beach even in winter. Similar to French, Spanish don't speak English either; so, mastering Spanish is an advantage here. It is also wise to travel to Portugal from here. Faro, Lagos, Lisbon, Sintra and Porto are some of the places to begin with. Mentioning Porto, one will think of Port wine, but the town itself has many very scenic views to offer.

Moving up north to Scandinavian countries, you will find a quite different landscape and culture. Denmark, Sweden, Finland, Norway, Iceland are in this category. They share some vocabulary in their languages but quite diverse in nature. Weather is colder, winter is longer and summer is shorter in this region. Culture wise, local population really appreciates and loves the sun. Sun bathing is very common and people try to avoid spending winter here. That is why air ticket is so expensive in winter. They are very polite, indirect and courteous in general unlike Dutch, German and French. Most people in Scandinavian countries speak very good English compared to the rest of Europe. A day visit in Copenhagen is far more than enough. Nothing much to see except sakura festival in summer. Stockholm consists of a wild part of Scottish archipelago, a dash of Neapolitan beach, not forgetting one or two gorgeous islands found in the vicinity; in the hardest granite rock to be found in Urals. Flocks of seagulls dancing with the breeze and where the fresh water meets the salty Baltic Sea promises beautiful scenery and landscapes. A white Christmas in Northern part of Stockholm, Kiruna is an enjoyable experience. Snow fights, land completely covered with snow (tundra), reindeer, husky dog sledge, snow mobile and watching northern lights or Aurora Borealis in the wilderness are really attractive and not to be missed. It took some bet and luck in the search of Aurora Borealis and it was really beautiful; just like the dynamic and moving sparkling stars in the lonely night. Another wonder of the world....

As for now, the journey of life continues, at least for another 4 years in Europe...

To all brigadiers out there; stand firm and be sure and steadfast in upholding the kingdom of God. Enjoy and treasure the times in The Boys' Brigade, learn as much as you can and push forward; far ahead... "Once a Brigadier, always a Brigadier"...

To all parents and church members, always remember this; support and encourage proactively the activities of The Boys' Brigade either financially or morally.

Thomas Moh
Reserved Lieutenant, 1st Sarikei Company.
The Boys' Brigade in Malaysia.

George Smith of the 2nd Sutton Coldfield asks Cpl Calvin Leung about life in the 37th Hong Kong

GS: What is the name of your Company?
CL: BBHK37th at The Evangelical Lutheran Church of Hong Kong Communion Lutheran Church.

GS: How many boys do you get on BB nights on average?
CL: Usually 20-25.

GS: What day of the week do you meet and for how long?
CL: Every Saturday afternoon 1500 to1800.

GS: Briefly run us through the structure of your BB meetings
CL: Full in, meeting of Christianity, to wear the badge (inspection), drill, dismiss.

GS: What is the highest badge attainable in your country, and have you got it?
CL: Founder's Badge, I have not got it.

GS: What is your favourite thing about BB?
CL: Friendship.

GS: What are the boys and the officers ranks?
CL: Brigader, Lance-Corporal, Corporal, Sergeant, Staff Sergeant.

GS: How is your Company structured in terms of age?
CL: Company section 12-20yrs.

GS: Do you do drill and if so how often?
CL: Every Saturday 1hour.

GS: What sports do your Company take part in at BB?
CL: Basketball, Handball, Football, Athletics.

GS: Is the uniform inspection strict at your Company?
CL: Yes.

GS: Which of the classes is your favourite?
CL: Sports.

GS: Is your Company the best Company in the world?
CL: I hope it will be the best in the world!

Josh Lawrence of the 2nd Sutton Coldfield asks How Kar Koh of the 39th Singapore some very interesting questions

JL. How many members do you have on average per week?
HK. The Company I'm currently in have 50 boys. Every week there's around 48 to 50 member coming for BB.

JL. Is your BB held within a City?
HK. Not really, BB in Singapore are held in schools. Mine is in Swiss Cottage Secondary School.

JL. How many miles do boys have to travel to get to BB?
HK. From less than 0.006 mile (10 Metres) to 18.6 miles (30 Kilometres).

JL. What day and time is it held?
HK. Friday 1430hr (SGT) And Saturday 0800hr (SGT).

JL. What colour is your uniform and do you wear a hat?
HK. Dark Blue and we do have field cap.

JL. Do you have drill every time you meet and for how long?
HK. Yes. 5 to 15 min of inspection.

JL. Do you have a band?
HK. Sadly no...

JL. Do you have a soccer team?
HK. No, but we do have soccer after parade on Saturday.

JL. Do you compete against other Companies?
HK. Yes we do.

JL. Do you do work to get your badges?
HK. Yes, every badge has it own criteria.

JL. What is the highest badge a boy can earn?
HK. The Founder's Man badge.

Josh receives the Queen's award from Captain Paul Arkinstall, July 2010.

JL. What sort of work do you need to do in order to achieve the highest badge?
HK. This is hard.... Let me slowly explain. The Founder's Man award is given to boys who are nominated by the officers, and passed the Founder's Man test. Boys who show good attitude, leadership, respect, responsibility, etc, have a better chance of getting it. Most of the time it is given to the top boys and most of them work hard throughout their 4 to 5 years! Example me!

JL. Is your Company linked to a church?
HK. Yes.

JL. Is it important that your BB turns up to the services?
HK. No. This also needs a bit of explanation. As you can see Singapore is a multi ethnic country and there are many different religions in Singapore, example Buddhism, the Christian, the Indian, Muslim and many more others. It is important for Singaporean to respect each other religion because of different practices and cultures. As for BB in Singapore, most of the boys are Buddhism and Christian, that is why the officers are not allowed to "force" them to go for services which may result to misunderstanding or disrespect for others. But if the boys want to attend the services, they are allowed to do so. Some of my friend they do attend services so it's not surprising. Further more the government encourage everyone to attend their religion activities.

JL Do you have an annual camp?
HK. We have some annual camps! The March camp where boys go through the solider training! The Life Skill where boys learn to cope their stress, the Expiation, where we walk around Singapore with map and compasses for 3 days and 2 nights!

JL. What is the food like?
HK. Nice! Especially the last night of every camp, that's always the best!

JL. What time do you need to get up for inspection at camp?
HK. Depend, some time is 5am, some time is 2.15am or latest is around 7am+.

JL. Is your BB the best in the world?
HK. If I say no, there won't be anything best for me any more!

JL. What is your favourite part of BB?
HK. When playing with my friends in BB. Because regardless of age, class, IQ and EQ Level, size, and etc, we just simply can't resist the fun we have together. Friendship is one of the strongest forces in my Company!

Something How Kar Koh also wanted to add was...
"My years in BB have changed me into a better person, getting to know new friends and picking up new skills that made me join this uniformed group. More importantly, it is the friendship that made this CCA look interesting, not the rankship".*

*CCA stands for Co-Curricular Activities. This is a programme or system for all Singapore schools. From Primary to Tertiary, the **CCA** consists these 4 categories. **Sports** – example basket ball, soccer etc. **Performing** – example Military band, choir, Chinese dance, drama etc. **Uniformed** group – example BB! GB, Scout etc. The last one is a **Club**, the Science club, English chest etc. In short we all call it CCA. **How Kar**

How Kar is one of our BB Singapore Founder Man this year. We in BB 39th Singapore Company have been doing well by moulding and shaping lives all these years. Currently, we have about 50 Boys, 7 primers and about 7 active officers. Boys are grouped in 4 squads.

The Boys enjoyed a wide range of activities. Besides the usual drill, first aid, outdoor cooking etc, our Boys just had a bowling session. We have inter-squad games regularly.

Chan Kwang San
Captain, BB 39th Singapore Company

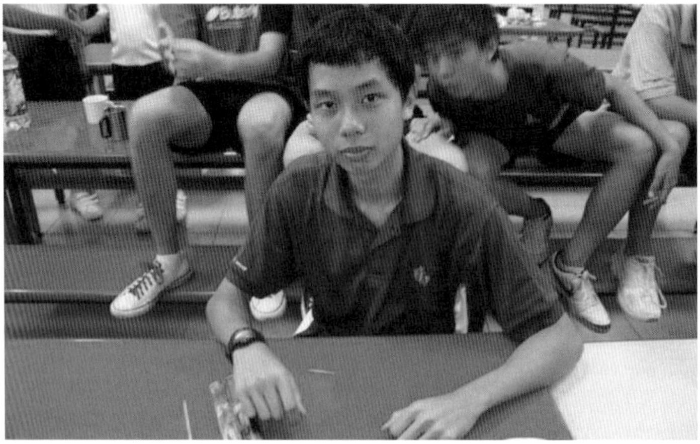

How Kar.

Newsboys!

The beginnings of our movement in Australia, taken from 'Boys, Urchins, Men: A History of The Boys' Brigade in Australia and Papua New Guinea 1882-1976' by M. E. Hoare. The extract below covers the 19th Century beginnings in Sydney.

In the early 1880s some civic-minded citizens and churchmen in Sydney became deeply worried about the 'condition of the lads engaged in street newspaper selling'. 'Ragged, shoeless, dirty, often hungry, and manifesting an ominous precocity in the adoption of the coarse and cunning habits which distinguish the outer fringe of society' the newspaper urchins or 'flippers' posed a problem for those concerned both with the 'moralities and decencies of life' among the young working-class people of central Sydney, and with the crime in the streets of the city.

The interested middle-class gentlemen of Sydney in 1882-84, successfully formed a 'brigade' or 'union' whose members 'should wear some sort of badge, and have something like a code of honour to sustain'. The leaders of this movement were J. R. Fairfax of the Sydney Morning Herald, A. S. Bennett of the Evening News and Dr James Jefferis of the Congregational Church, Pitt Street, a well- known Sydney clergyman.

The first experiment in 1882 was not an immediate success and was soon reorganised into a Newsboys' Brigade and Young Workmen's Club for fourteen to twenty-one year olds, meeting initially in premises at the corner of Sussex and Liverpool Streets, Sydney, and then to the Old Baptist Chapel in Elizabeth Street. Sir James Martin, the Chief Justice of New South Wales, became head of the organising committee, which commenced a band and gymnasium, and a small library. The work was, indeed, at first held up to some ridicule by the rival Daily Telegraph but in Jefferis it had a powerful and determined defender.

By 1890-91 the organisation had rented headquarters and a gymnasium at 390 Sussex Street, Sydney, and boasted powerful support from its president, Sir Frederick M. Darley, Martin's successor as Chief Justice, and the trustees and officers, J. R. Fairfax, George Lewis, E. D. Gray and F. Bender. The Lady Mayoress of Sydney was head of a ladies' organising committee and the full-time superintendent, Mr Cleland was responsible for a seven-night weekly programme consisting of gymnasium, carbine and cutlass drill, brass band and a 'minstrel troupe' catering for an enrolment of some 350 Boys and a fluctuating nightly attendance of from 40 to 150.

The early nineties were very troubled times for Australia as strikes grew, banks collapsed and the economy generally waned. The waterfront was especially prone to trouble in Sydney and so the 'Boys' Brigade' of Sussex Street found itself providing 400 beds (one night's accommodation) and 1,000 meals in 1890-91 for homeless and hungry Boys of the city. Socials were also run and an employment service begun. Under these circumstances the movement readily received the active support of all leading churchmen, including 'Rabbi' Alexander Barnard Davis and the Anglican Primate.

By 1892-93 the 'Boys' Brigade' had moved to 22 and 24 Campbell Street, Haymarket, Sydney, where by 1894-95 it had a gymnasium fourteen by twenty-four metres; a general recreation room, library and reading room; class rooms and sleeping accommodation. Both the Mayor of Sydney and Justice Matthew Henry Stephen were prominent as vice- presidents in the 'Brigade', which in 1895 had an enrolment of 300 and nightly attendance of 60 to 175.

The most significant development for the history of The Boys' Brigade International, however, was the adoption by the Sydney organisation before 1894 of The Boys' Brigade Object as laid down by Smith in the United Kingdom and elsewhere. In the Annual Report of the Sydney Boys' Brigade of 1894-95 great stress was laid upon the BB Object and the 'traditional' method.

At the Campbell Street centre in the mid-nineties Mr and Mrs Spear, the full-time superintendent and matron, presided over a busy programme of activities designed to promote 'Reverence, Reality and Religion', the Sydney Boys' Brigade's own brand of the '3-Rs'. On Sundays Mrs H. T. Robjohns conducted a well-attended Bible Class which in 1893 had an enrolment of 250, and in 1895-96 recorded an average attendance of forty to forty-five 'Juniors'. One more step in the direction of The Boys' Brigade as conceived by Smith was the attendance of a drill instructor, firstly Sergeant Cuddy and then Staff Colour- Sergeant Munson, to maintain 'that discipline and spirit of obedience which may be deemed an essential feature in the proper management of the Brigade'. Classes in physiology and natural history also bespoke more traditional BB activities. In 1892-93 nightshelter was provided for 1,100 to 1,200 Boys and some 700 meals were served, and one dozen were found employment.

There can be little doubt that the 'Sydney Newsboys' Brigade' as it was known from the outset, was greatly and positively influenced in the mid 1890s by the successful introduction of William Smith's ideas from Britain. The formation of the first more traditional BB Companies in Melbourne (1891), Perth (1895), Launceston (1897), Hobart (1898), Mackay (1897), Brisbane (1898) and Adelaide (1899) received relatively good coverage in some of the religious and secular press of the period and Smith's ideas were given a good airing in the similar journals coming from Britain, and reports of the British movement were certainly not unknown in the Australian press. By 1895-96 the Newsboys' Brigade had nearly 400 members (ten to eighteen years old) under the new superintendent and matron, Mr and Mrs C. Thackeray, and by then had moved its headquarters yet again to 184 Elizabeth Street, Sydney, which premises were opened by Lady Hampden, wife of the Governor, on 22 October 1896. One special feature of the work was still the 'Brigade Labour Bureau'.

Two years later, in the Report for 1897-98, the Newsboys' Brigade proclaimed its 'prime basis' as one of the 'broadest Christianity, without cant or affectation' and in 1899 was still affirming its allegiance to the 'British Boys' Brigade' Object. At the same time the Sydney Brigade set forth some clear practical aims: to keep Boys off the streets by providing instruction and amusement; to encourage honesty, sobriety, self-respect and industry; to assist in finding employment, and to bring Boys under 'beneficient influences' and provide them with a good start in life. Proof that the work was succeeding was given when two of the organisation's own former members became honorary assistant managers in 1897-98. Thackeray was superintendent from September 1895 until August 1897, although by this time the membership had dropped to 200, with an average attendance of 100.

In 1898-99 the newsboys' organisation took stock of sixteen years' work. Throughout that time the occupations of its 'inmates' had remained identical: newsboys, factory lads, rag and bone pickers, bootblacks, lace and knick-knack sellers and the general 'juvenile element' of the street. It is not hard to imagine that the faithful, indomitable Mrs Robjohns must have had the occasional difficult task in her Sunday evening classes or that the 'Sol-Fa Singing' class of 1893 must have had its more critical moments, as well as the circus visits and reception of 550 newsboys by the Governor, the Earl of Jersey, at Government House.

In 1899 the standard of 'musical drill' in the Newsboys' Brigade was considered high enough for the activity to be demonstrated at Government House along with a 'Fancy Drill Squad', upon which no further comment is given!

With thanks to Neil Hawthorn,
BB 7th Victoria Kerang & 1st Victoria Armadale

The BB front cover logo

When I asked for BB guys around the world to design the logo for the book cover, a few excellent ideas were received. Here are two very different ideas that didn't quite make the cover – but are too good to miss out altogether! The design on the left was created by Chris Wall and the image on the right was produced by Kayleigh Overton.

The Changing Face of BB in New Zealand

Within 3 years of William Smith starting BB, New Zealand, a British Colony on the other side of the world commenced BB. This was in 1886 when the first NZ Company, 1st Christchurch commenced but it was not until 1926 that NZ Companies like the 1st Dunedin and many other Companies in both the North and South Islands were properly established leading eventually to forming our own National Brigade Dominion Council in 1931 with a full time Secretary.

In 1936 BBNZ had grown to 74 Companies and 47 Life Boy teams with a total roll of 1,268 Boys for The BB and 791 Life Boys.

From the 1930's BB Week was a popular way of funding, with various percentages of the proceeds being retained by Headquarters and the remainder returned to the local Company. BB Week no longer exists as a means of national funding for BB in NZ.

BB HQ and the local Battalions were very strong on leadership training. From the late 40's, numerous training courses were operating throughout NZ for Officers and NCO's.

In 1956 a job offer was made to Alford Dornan, the Training Organiser for the BB in Northern Ireland to take up the position of Training and Extension Officer in NZ. The structure of the Movement in NZ was similar to that in Northern Ireland having a rural and urban population in smallish settlements.

Training in NZ for Officers and NCO's was taken to a new level and our membership peaked during the 1960's to a total of 12,300 in 255 Companies and 232 Life Boy Teams.

National Leadership Development Stage 1 & 2 Courses of 8 days duration, held in the South Islands Nelson Lakes National Park are still popular today and a requirement for the Queen's Award.

Award programmes in NZ were structured on those in the UK and in 1945 the first NZ badge revision was undertaken to review the suitability of all awards for NZ conditions.

Over the years new awards and programmes have been adopted to work with the present sections that form a Company. Today's programmes & awards are now very different especially in the Company Section.

Anchor Boy Section – Ages 6 to 7 (years 2 and 3 at school)
Activities are ... having fun. There is a programme of games, activities and singing. Anchor Boys are encouraged to attend Sunday School or Church.

Team Section – Ages 8 to 11 (years 4 to 7)
Activities are ... having more fun. The programme has five parts – spiritual, physical, community, educational and adventure. It includes games, figure marching, crafts, music and the Achievement Scheme. You can earn 6 awards, the last and most important being the Gold Achievement Badge.

Company Section – Ages 11 to 18 (years 7 to 14 plus)
The Company has two programmes with interesting activities that will allow you to enjoy yourself and learn new skills. The first part, called the **FUN** programme (for years 7 to 10) is followed by the **RISC** programme (for years 10 onwards).

The **FUN** awards give you a taste of the wide variety of interesting activities that your Company Section may run and that will help you to achieve the President's Award.

The **RISC** awards are for seniors who want to be challenged to take chosen activities to a new level. **RISC** awards fit in with the Young New Zealand Challenge award that is recognised throughout the world. By doing the **RISC** programme and registering for the YNZC you can gain the BB Queen's Award and YNZC Gold, two major awards at the same time.

By the start of the 21st Century membership of Boys' Brigade NZ was around 2400 with National Executive concerned over difficulty in starting new Companies. In 2003 BBNZ launched a new church missionary outreach programme called ICONZ Adventure for school year boys 4 to 7.

ICONZ is a new skin over the existing bones of BB, sharing the same aims and object. The programme is designed for kiwi kids to become NZ icons with catchy award names like Tycoonz, Bushmanz, Legendz.

ICONZ Anchor – Ages 6 to 7 (years 2 and 3 at school)
ICONZ Adventure – Ages 8 to 11 (years 4 to 7) Operational from 2004
ICONZ Xtreme – Ages 11 to 14 (years 7 plus). Operational from 2009.
ICONZ Ultimate – Ages 14+ (years 11 plus).

You will find ICONZ units appearing throughout NZ. At times they will take part in local competitions or activities that Companies have organised.

ICONZ units and your Company Section are all part of one organisation: Boys' Brigade in NZ. Go to our BBNZ Website www.bb.org.nz for more information.

In 2009, BBNZ with ICONZ is making a strong and positive comeback by taking the lead in youth outreach ministry for Churches. The re-birthing of BB in NZ with the ICONZ brand equals the interest and enthusiasm that our founder would have experienced when he first started in 1883. The growth of ICONZ has a bright future for BB in NZ.

Les Bouterey
BBNZ President

Collecting BB Memorabilia

It's a fact that when Boys leave the BB, the BB doesn't leave them. The affection in which the Brigade is held means that quite often some bits of personal BB history are retained as memories of good times. Small items gained with effort and worn with pride, such as badges, are easily kept and stored, as are the famous BB Membership Cards, often described as 'little works of art'. Certificates and other types of memorabilia including uniform items, photographs etc are also popular.

Most *collectables* are usually small and with some degree of rarity, but it helps if they are physically attractive. The Old BB badges, introduced from 1885, but particularly those used until 1968, were especially collected since they were silver in colour and clearly represented the activity for which they were awarded; for instance the 'Bugler's Badge' was in the shape of a traditional hunting horn 'bugle'.

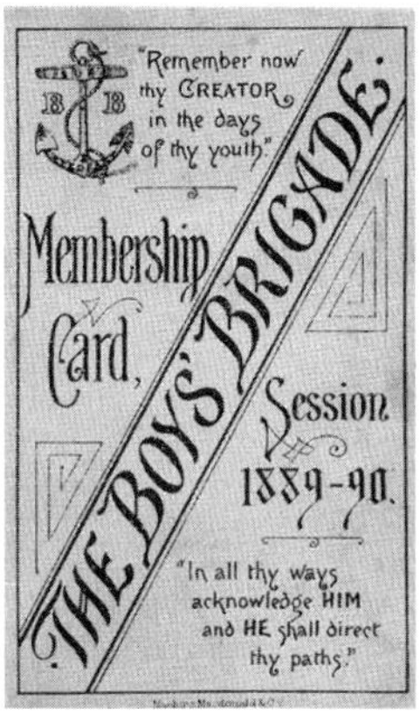

1889-90 Membership Card.

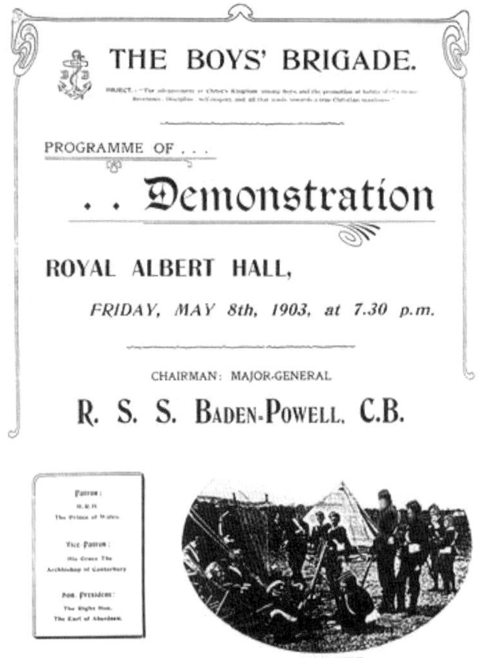
THE BOYS' BRIGADE.

PROGRAMME OF . . .

. . Demonstration

ROYAL ALBERT HALL,

FRIDAY, MAY 8th, 1903, at 7.30 p.m.

CHAIRMAN: MAJOR-GENERAL

R. S. S. BADEN-POWELL, C.B.

A CAMP SCENE.

Display Programme 1903.

A young Edwardian BB boy.

Souvenir jug from 1927 Camp.

BB Scout badge.

With 126 years of history to its name, the BB has a long run of consecutive membership cards, differing patterns of uniform, certificates, badges and the like.

The collecting instinct is strong in the nature of many folk, so when they are ex-BB or perhaps still currently serving, it's not surprising that there are 'BB Collectors' out there.

The official 'BB Badge Collectors' Club' was started in 1982 by the then Brigade Archivist Miss Muriel Ellis, and a magazine was published. In the years leading up to the BB Centenary in 1983 a number of publications edited by Muriel were published by the Brigade, culminating in a quite well-produced professionally printed 'Archive Series' in time for the Centenary. The 'Badges' publication, whilst limited, was the most widely used of these booklets and certainly led to collectors, for the first time perhaps, looking to get one of everything for their collection. The 'Knowledge', is the one thing that collectors crave.

1960s badges.

Sources of memorabilia in the 1980s were limited to dusty cupboards and storerooms in ancient churches and chapels, or attics of ancient BB Officers and their relatives. It soon became quite common to see BB Badges and similar items appearing at Antique fairs and later

The New BBUK Company Senior Section badges.

specialist 'Collectors Fairs'. Prices of course, were quite variable since most of the sellers, with a few exceptions, hadn't got any knowledge of what they were selling. Common badges were often being marketed at 'rip-off' prices with rare badges going for a song. Muriel Ellis, now Muriel Gibbs, was made redundant by the BB in 1986, so the popular 'Archive Series' booklets proved to be the last of such publications by the Brigade – however the genie was out of the bottle! In the 1990s it became clear that for badges at least, a much more comprehensive 'Guide' would need to be produced. The Badge Collectors Club was re-started in 1994, and the 'Newsletter' was produced again. Mr Bob Mandry was the co-ordinator, and the volunteers had taken over where the professional archivist had left-off. The BB Badge Collectors Club changed its name to the 'BB Collectors' Club in 2001, reflecting the widening of collecting interests among its members. The BB Collectors Club magazine was now being mailed to hundreds of members. There was even an annual 'Collectors' Club' badge to collect! But what made this 'General BB Memorabilia' collecting so popular? The answer is quite simple and can be summed-up in one word 'eBay'.

In the late 1990s and into the 21st Century the collecting of BB Memorabilia was 'booming'. Two BB officers, Mr Allan Percival and Mr Ken King – Allan a serving full-time BB staff member at the time, and Ken a former full-time BB staff member – introduced a series of 'BB Memorabilia Auctions' to raise cash for the BB in the developing world. These auctions held at BB HQ and other locations throughout the UK, were quite profitable. They were held up to three times a year and continued into 2008. Auctions were also run through the Collectors' Club at a number of venues. There was a BB Memorabilia Auction held at Brigade Council in 2008, a tradition started at the Council in Durham in 1991. The BB Collectors Club even had its own column in the 'BB Gazette' for some years. However, it was the on-line 'eBay' auction which would eventually out perform all other sources of material.

The need for a comprehensive 'Badge' book was met with the publication in 2000 of 'Badges of the Brigade', a collaboration of effort from three stalwarts of the Collectors' Club, Rob Bolton, Bob Mandry and Les Howie with assistance from Mr David Aubrey Q.C. Badges of the Brigade took collecting badges on to a whole new plane having star 'rarity values' included as well as colour pictures of every BB badge produced in the UK. The book was well received, and since no other organisation had a similar reference work, the interest in collecting BB badges increased even more.

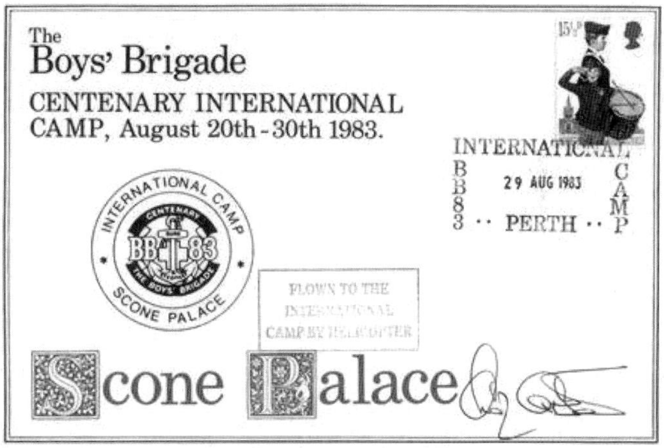

1st Day Cover. International Camp, Scone Palace.

A BB Collectors Club Website was set-up by Mr Kevin Aitchison which used images and material from 'Badges of the Brigade'. In 2005 when Bob Mandry reduced his involvement with the Collectors' Club, it was Kevin who became joint-co-ordinator, then the new editor of the Club quarterly 'Newsletter', and eventually principal co-ordinator of the Club in 2007. The Club now offers a 'New Badge' service for members who want to purchase the latest badges to be issued – a service started by Bob and continued by Kevin. A glance through a Collectors' Club Newsletter over the years would provide an insight into the many facets of BB collecting today, which is very much more than 'memorabilia', since it covers the whole 126 years of the Brigade. Articles have been published on medals, bugles, postcards, books, scent cards, other brigades, scouting, stamps, covers, membership cards, photographs, programmes ... etc.

For some BB 'Collectors' the main interest is not simply 'collecting'. The focus is upon the rich 'family history' of the BB of which they were or still are a part. The place of the Brigade in the history of the British nation and its spread all over the world to countries of the Commonwealth and beyond provides seemingly endless scope for research.

Robin Bolton, President, Wolverhampton Battalion, UK
Author of *Badges of The Boys' Brigade*

The BB in Africa

Africa is a massive continent, but where the British Empire touched it the Boys' Brigade had a foothold. Initially, what is now the Republic of South Africa was the place where the BB grew strongly, not only in the British Colonies but also in the Boer republics, with fifty Companies formed between 1889 and 1899. Unfortunately as war broke out in 1899 and the twentieth century arrived, the BB in South Africa was overwhelmed by the Cadet Movement. Elsewhere in the Continent in the 1890s and early 1900s isolated Companies were established in present-day Ghana, Nigeria, Malawi, Kenya, and even in Egypt!

BB Growth in the African continent really started after World War II and was quite spectacular in the 1950s and 60s in such populous countries as Nigeria. Whilst it has not been a story of steady development in every country, mainly due to internal conflicts and some natural disasters, there is today a thriving BB movement in many African countries. Some countries such as Swaziland and Congo DCR have their own Christian Brigades similar to the BB. The BB is 'Regionalised' now and sometimes includes Girls' Brigade. In East Africa it is present in Burundi, Kenya, Rwanda, Tanzania & Uganda. In Southern Africa it is in Lesotho, Malawi, Zambia and Zimbabwe. In West Africa, Benin, Cameroon, Cote D'Ivoire, Gambia, Ghana, Nigeria, Sierra Leone and Togo all have their own BB. In the 1950s and 60s the BB was organised very much like the parent organisation in the UK 'implanted' into Africa, but with the 'wind of change' and national independence arriving from the late 1950s the BB has managed to become much more 'Africanized' adapting to local needs in a way that generally never happened in North America.

Rob Bolton

The BB in South Africa

The first South African Company was formed in 1889 in Natal. The 1st Pietermaritzburg and the 1st Cape Town lasted only a short while, but in 1892 more companies sprung up around South Africa, including around 50 in Cape, Natal and Boer republics. The 1st Umsinga Company was formed at the Gordon Memorial Mission in Zululand.

The BB was popular in the Transual due to a high British population. The BB is still going strong today. See www.bbsa.org for more information.

The above was taken from the BBSA website and was the very last piece produced for Planet BB – the night before printing. We just had enough space to fit it in!

Christian Children's Centre Uganda

The Christian Children's Centre Uganda is a charity organization founded by a native Ugandan, Grace Wamala, in 2003. Grace began working at the Namirembe Cathedral in Kampala teaching music and Bible study to the Boys and Girls Brigade, a youth development group. This work inspired him to reach out to orphans and street kids in the community in order to help them get off the street, and become responsible and self-supporting individuals. His goal was to accomplish this through mentoring, motivational speaking, and providing shelter.

About Grace Wamala

Grace was born in 1986 in Kampala, Uganda. His father left the family when Grace was 8 years old, and he grew up with his mother and 6 other siblings. The family was very poor, and Grace, being the oldest boy, was responsible for finding work and providing food for the family. During this time, Grace had negative influences from other boys and got involved with drugs, often spending the money he made on this instead of food for the family. He would often stay out late, and was spending less and less time supporting the family. Because of this, his mother sent him to stay with one of the founders of the Boys' and Girls' Brigade at the Namirembe Cathedral, Mr Kashangirwe, hoping that religious influence and community involvement would put him back on the right path. This was when he was 10 years old.

During the next several years, Grace became involved with the Church choir, the Brigade, and eventually was teaching music to the Brigade and holding Bible classes. Over this time, Grace was motivated to contribute to the community, renew his support of the family, and to be a positive influence on the lives of troubled youth. Through Church, he did outreach to community children, providing food, clothing, and health information on topics such as AIDS. In order to do this sort of outreach, a valid government-issued organization certificate is required.

Poultry project at the orphanage.

When he was 18, Grace's father had built a house, and invited Grace and his brothers to live in it by way of an apology for abandoning them. Grace moved into this house and later founded the Christian Children's Home Uganda (CCHU), in order to acquire a community based organization (CBO) certificate to allow him to do community outreach. Upon the founding of CCHU, Grace began networking in the community by reaching out to community members; giving Bible classes, parenting advice, promoting good hygiene, raising health awareness, and teaching skills for personal support.

With CCHU as a CBO, Grace was able to take in several street orphans and provide them with shelter and constant support. i.e. food, education, and shelter. Since then, Grace's aspirations have strengthened, and continued to motivate him to be a positive influence on the lives of street orphans. Currently, Grace is responsible for 54 children at the renamed CCCU and is struggling financially. Planet BB has already sent over £500 to support the orphanage. See Facebook groups for full details.

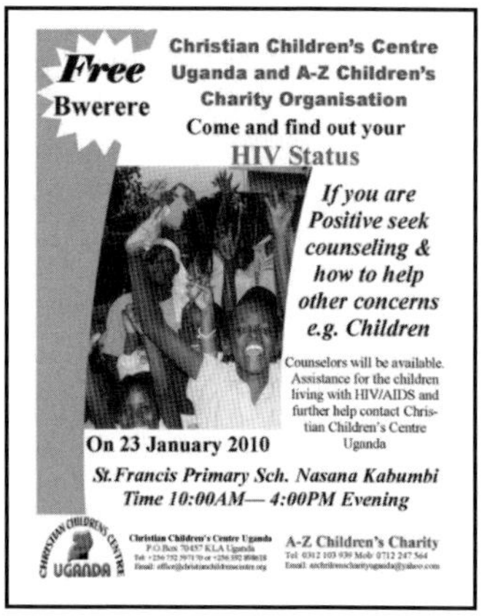

HIV testing and counselling at CCCU.

THE BB HYMN is sung at BB companies all over the world!

Will your anchor hold in the storms of life,
When the clouds unfold their wings of strife?
When the strong tides lift, and the cables strain,
Will your anchor drift or firm remain?

We have an anchor that keeps the soul
Steadfast and sure while the billows roll;
Fastened to the rock which cannot move,
Grounded firm and deep in the Saviours love.

Will your anchor hold in the straits of fear,
When the breakers roar and the reef is near?
While the surges rave and the wild winds blow,
Shall the angry waves then your bark o'erflow?

Will your anchor hold in the floods of death,
When the waters cold chill your latest breath?
On the rising tide you can never fail,
While your anchor holds within the veil.

Will your eyes behold through the morning light,
The city of gold and the harbour bright?
Will you anchor safe by the heavenly shore
When life's storms are past for evermore?

Priscilla J Owens 1882

Towards a True Christian Manliness

A History of The Boys' Brigade in Zimbabwe 1948 – 2008

"Of Southern Rhodesia itself it may be said that it seems a very healthy and pleasant place for the European Settler... Salisbury and Bulawayo are spaciously laid out and in many part beautiful. The country in between is mainly monotonous and sparsely populated veldt covered with small trees and scrub. There is a wild grandeur, however, about the Matopos, and the World's View is a fitting resting place for a man of the outstanding personality and vision of Cecil Rhodes... As regards the Rhodesian Churches finding in the BB a useful instrument, a number of ex-members and other interested are now exploring the possibilities in the white community, which is not large, numbering only 55000, the majority of whom are to be found in Salisbury and Bulawayo. The small coloured community, some 3000 in number, is without any type of Boys' work and there may be a sphere for the BB, while the native population of over a million has Pathfinder Scouts at most of the missionary centres."

William McVicker, Overseas BB Secretary, December 1939

Ten years after William McVicker's tour of Southern Africa, and following the devastating ravages of the Second World War in Europe, the British Government was promoting the immigration of settlers to Southern Rhodesia. It was as a result of this post war immigration that the 1st Bulawayo Company was founded at the Main Street Methodist Church in Bulawayo, followed closely by the 1st Wankie Company in 1949, and the 1st Salisbury in 1950. Whilst the two city based Companies catered for European Boys, the 1st Wankie Company was based within the mining compound of the Wankie colliery and catered exclusively for African Boys. The early BB Companies followed a strictly British format, following closely the regulations and uniform of the BB in the UK, however local situations required some change to uniform and awards regulations, in particular the camping badge. The 1st Salisbury Companies strict adherence to the UK system ensured that by 1955, they were able to award Queen's Badges, and continued to do so on a yearly basis until the late 1960s.

Nationally, growth was slow, and even though efforts were made at starting a National administration, to promote and administer the work of the BB in Southern Rhodesia, the enrolment of Companies and Officers still remained within the realms of the Brigade Overseas Secretary in London. Following the closure of the 1st Wankie Company sometime in the early 1950s, it was not until the formation of the 2nd Salisbury Company to cater for Boys in the coloured community of Arcadia, that BB work started to flourish, this was followed soon after with the formation of the 3rd, 4th and 5th Salisbury Companies, and by the mid 1960s, the formation of the 1st QueQue Company and 1st Morgenster Companies was the start of prolific work in the rural areas, particularly amongst the Reformed Church.

The 'winds of change' of Harold McMillan's Government was granting many of Britain's Colonies independence, and by 1960 this was rapidly spreading across Africa. The dissolution of the Federation of Rhodesia and Nyasaland, mean that both Nyasaland and Northern Rhodesia were granted independence. In the case of Nyasaland, which had become the independent state of Malawi, this was the death of the BB, which had been flourishing since 1911, as the government sponsored Malawi Pioneers became the prescribed youth organisation for all Malawian youth. Southern Rhodesia became known as Rhodesia, and was not granted independence as Britain felt they did not meet the requirements politically. The BB worldwide was following a similar route, with eventual autonomy in Brigade matters being established through the creation on the World Conference. The BB in Rhodesia formally set up a Council in 1960, and started to develop an independent administration which become necessary following sanctions imposed on the country in the late 1960s after the Declaration of Independence by Ian Smith in 1965.

Initially this had little impact on the BB in Rhodesia, however as sanctions were tightened, the supply of uniforms, publications and awards became difficult, and eventually led to the manufacture of most items by the 1970s. The declaration of a Republic in 1970, meant that the Queen was no longer recognised as head of state, and because of this the Queen's Badges was replaced by the Founder's badge, however the bush war had intensified by the mid 1970s, and as a result, many of the Companies were no longer able to provide awards programmes which was necessary to meet the requirements of the award of the Founder's badge. The first award of this was only 1979, and included the locally developed awards structure which was introduced in 1976, using locally manufactured badges, and handbooks. Further developments included the introduction of a pre-junior section known as the Anchor section, and an awards program based on that in use by the Junior Section.

By the mid 1970s the Brigade in Rhodesia was the fifth strongest numerically in the world, with 90 percent of this membership in the rural areas amongst the African Reformed Church, however the intensified war meant that by independence, membership had dropped to a few city based Companies with a combined strength of less than 900 Boys. The post independence era was one of uncertainty, many of the white families that had remained, left the country further depleting the ranks of Boys and Officers in the few remaining city based BB Companies.

By the late 1980s a concerted effort of training and Company formation, particularly amongst the Salvation Army, meant that Brigade membership was approximately 1800 Boys and Officers in 65 Companies around the country, with the focus of the work being directed towards the Reformed Church and the Rural Masvingo Companies in the early 1990s. Brigade extension work began to flourish in Bulawayo and the Matableleand Province following the employment of full-time field training staff, this was evident in the growth in this area in the mid to late 1990s, an area which had been particularly weak. As much of Brigade work was being focused toward rural and high density residential areas, uniform and published material was adapted to cater for the shift in focus, particularly with the introduction of an Agriculture Scheme in 1986, and then subsequently the safety and Health programs in 1994. The agriculture scheme, which included the running of income generating projects within rural Companies, was particularly successful in the rural Companies of the Masvingo province, however, drought and the weakening economy was effecting the financial viability of the projects, forcing some to close by the end of the 1990s. The presence of Girls in many Companies, prompted Brigade Council to adopt resolution which allowed the inclusion of Girls in the Brigade from 1996. Whilst the organisation remained primarily for Boys, the provision allowed for the recognition and inclusion of Girls, something which had been going on unofficially for a number of years.

The 50th Anniversary in 1998, was a far cry from the massive 40th anniversary celebrations, as the BB was in decline. The country was in the middle of political and economic turmoil, which only preceded the farm invasions and massive inflation and economic turmoil of the mid 2000s. By mid 2004 it was assumed that only one BB Company continued to operate, albeit without BB uniform, for fear of political retribution, and the term Brigade was now too closely associated with the government sponsored Youth Brigade which was a primary force of intimidation for the ruling political party.

Whilst other Companies may occasionally report Brigade activities the total collapse of any form of national administration and council, along with the difficulties in communication and transport, caused by the collapse of the economy has meant that little or no information can be established as to the state of any other BB work apart from the one operating Company in the capital, Harare.

Colin Swinton, author of the History of the BB in Zimbabwe, 2009

1st Acomb (York) Boys' Brigade has a link with 1st Begoro Boys' Brigade Company in the Fanteakwa region of Ghana

In February 2003 Reverend Tony Hand, the vicar of the Church of the Holy Redeemer in Acomb, York received a letter from Kathleen Howard, a local woman, who had lived in Ghana for many years whilst her husband undertook missionary service out there. Peter Howard had been to preach at Holy Redeemer and was reminded that we have a Boys' Brigade Company there. Kathleen wrote that she knew that The Boys' Brigade was very strong across many denominations in Ghana and wondered if 1st Acomb would be interested in corresponding with boys overseas.

Reverend Hand passed the letter to our Captain, Ian Clarkson, and we agreed that we would be interested in forming a link, as this would help our boys towards a better understanding of other cultures and support them in the international award work. In February 2004 we received a letter from Mike Yeboah, Chair of the Fanteakwa-York Community Link and member of the Elders of the Presbyterian Church in Begoro, confirming interest in forming a link between 1st Begoro Boys' and Girls' Brigade and 1st Acomb Boys' Brigade.

We have been corresponding through letters with the Company in Ghana for a few years now, but since our first letters in 2004 there have been many changes. Originally when we began writing Evans was their captain, however for unknown reasons he fled the town and took a lot of the Boys' Brigade equipment including, uniforms, colours and band instruments. However, the Elders of the Presbyterian Church (similar to Church council) wanted to ensure the continuation of the Brigade for the young people of Begoro. They appointed a new captain, Emmanuel Annor-Kwei who has begun re-building the Company and so far been very successful. The Elders provided funding for new uniforms and colours.

Company Programme

The programme of 1st Begoro Company is in many ways very similar to our programme at 1st Acomb (York). They do drill using exactly the same instruction book as we do; however, their interpretation of the book is slightly different. For example we march bringing our arms to 45 degrees whereas they march bringing their arms level with their shoulders. They also do Bible study classes as we do, music, singing and dancing are also part of their programme. However, due to lack of resources, activities are somewhat restricted and the Company does not operate the badge awards scheme.

Also the electricity supply in Ghana is unreliable and therefore if it is not working they cannot meet as they only have the church available for their meetings, there are no other rooms for them. Recently the Brigade has acquired a large building near to the church, however the building is currently derelict and as they have little funds they will struggle to clear the building and make into a place where they could meet for the brigade sessions. Therefore as part of our link with Begoro we would like to help them raise funds to help them with their project.

Ghana – 1st Acomb visits 1st Begoro

In 2005 officers from 1st Acomb Company decided they would like to try and raise the funds to enable Seniors from the Company to visit Ghana to find out more about BB over there. We held many fundraising events such as a sponsored Stepathon, a Race Night, table top sales, indoor ice skating and lots of other activities. We also applied for grants from local charitable trusts, Yorkash – the local youth grant scheme, Manor School, York Children's Trust and the National Lottery Awards for All. It took two years to raise sufficient money for the visit.

In August 2007 the seniors from 1st Acomb spent 10 days in Begoro. This was a significant year, since 2007 marked the 200th Anniversary of the Abolition of Slavery in Britain and the 50th Anniversary of Ghanaian Independence.

We shared in many BB activities as well as visiting the local area to learn about their society, economy and culture. Our programme was as follows:

Friday 10 – BB dancing at Presby welcome service.

Friday:	Visit to the Chief of Fanteakwa Region Visit to the Chief Executive Officer of Begoro Visit to the Church Elders Begoro market
Saturday:	Visit to Trudu Falls, Begoro Company Drill (1st Acomb and 1st Begoro joint) Ghanaian wedding
Sunday:	Church Football tournament
Monday:	Visit to Dedeso and Lake Volta
Tuesday:	Hike to Mount Sekune Visit to Presbyterian Secondary School, Begoro Evening Drumming in Church
Wednesday:	Visit to Osino, Batik Factory – made batik cloth Visit to Abompe, Bead Factory
Thursday:	Visit to Danso, Teak Plantation, Begoro Visit to Begoro Water Works. Evening film show of 1st Begoro Enrolment Service and dedication of the Colours
Friday:	Visit to Bunso, National Arboretum Visit to the National Cocoa Research Institute, New Tafo
Saturday:	Visit to the Patrons and to share with them our thoughts on how we can work together with 1st Begoro Company in the future.
Sunday:	Church Parade Evaluation Meeting with Church Elders – drafting of Memorandum of Understanding Evening 1st Begoro song and dance entertainment
Monday:	Visit to Aburi Crafts market Journey home

When we returned we made presentations and a webpage to help others see our experiences and help them gain awards in international award.

Saturday 11 – 1st Acomb & 1st Begoro BB Drill 2.

Friday 17 – 1st Acomb and 1st Begoro BB bus trip to Bunso, N.

Sunday 19 – 1st Acomb & 1st Begoro at Church Parade.

Sunday 19 – BB Colour Party.

Tuesday 14 – Hiking to Sekune Mountain.

Sunday 19 – Company Captains.

The Future

We have signed a Memorandum of Understanding outlining the future of our link and agreeing how we will work together to ensure the survival of the Boys' Brigade in Begoro, York and throughout the world.

Both Companies are now continuing fundraising to raise money for a reciprocal visit of officers and young people from 1st Begoro Company to visit York and to enable them to complete their community building.

Other Companies

Whilst our contact has been largely with 1st Begoro Company we are aware of other Companies in Ghana. We met with the Captain of the Boys' Brigade at New Tafo and there is certainly a BB Company in the Accra Cantonments, however we do not currently have contact details for them.

One of the biggest difficulties in forming a link with African communities is the issue of communication. Many people in Ghana have mobile phones, but transmitters are few and far between and there is no reception in most of the country. Similarly, email access is available but in Begoro, non-payment of rent means that communication is regularly suspended – consequently email correspondence between our Captain and theirs relies on Emmanuel's occasional visits to an internet café in Accra or Kumasi. Written correspondence is the most effective means of communication but takes a long time and Ghanaian people have to pay for PO box services in order to receive their mail.

Memorandum of Understanding between 1st Begoro Girls' and Boys' Brigades and 1st Acomb Boys' Brigade

The Boys' and Girls' Brigades are non-profit making organisations and while they have charitable status they are not at liberty to make monetary donations. This agreement made between them refers to two independently run and funded brigades.

The below are the areas and projects that both 1st Begoro Girls' and Boys' Brigade and 1st Acomb Boys' Brigade agree to pursue and develop.

Develop reciprocal visits between the brigade leaders and members, funding will be the responsibility of each individual Company.

Yearly projects on a mutually agreed theme. 1st years theme = Friendship Banners.

Yearly exchange of a sample of handicrafts as completed in Brigade sessions.

Completion of a diary of events, records of achievement and ideas on each week's programme, to be exchanged termly.

Exchange of wider Brigade publications and materials.

Continuation of 2-way communication between boys/girls and boys through the central church.

All work completed under the link will help to ensure the survival of the Boys' and Girls' Brigade both in Begoro, York and throughout the world, while also contributing to the individual girls and boys awards.

Signed by and on 20th August 2007

Emmanuel Annor Kwei	Hannah Abboah – Offei	Lynn Davies
Captain	Captain	Captain
1st Begoro Boys' Brigade	1st Begoro Girls' Brigade	1st Acomb Boys' Brigade

How the BB came to Nigeria

The awareness of The Boys' Brigade in Nigeria started in 1906 at Lagos. It was introduced by Mr (later Canon) Wakeman, a staff of the CSS bookshop. He established the first Company in Nigeria at the Holy Trinity Anglican Church Ebute-Ero in the then capital Lagos state on September 5th 1908, and was registered in London with Rev Thomas A.J. Ogunbiyi of the same church as the first Chaplain. From such humble beginnings The Boys' Brigade began to spread like wild fire to other parts of the country. First Lagos Battalion was inaugurated on 12th August 1965, Ikeja Council, still in Lagos, was inaugurated in May 1969. The growth of the BB in Nigeria from 1908-1961 was in three dimensions in the Western, Northern and South/East. BB was introduced to the Southern region of Nigeria at Shagamu Methodist Church by Rev and Mrs W.F. Mellon. It came to the Northern region in 1935 at St. George Anglican Church Zaria, then to South/East Nigeria in 1936 at Bannham Memorial Methodist Church Agri road Port Harcourt. On 19th April 1961 the first meeting of all the regions was held at Ilorin Kwara state giving birth to the National Council of The Boys' Brigade with Rt Rev I.O.S. Okunsanya as the first president, and Rev S.O. Mariyesa as the first National Secretary. The Boys' Brigade celebrated its Centenary Anniversary last year with a host of activities all through the year and a service in the Church where the first Company was formed. The numeric strength of membership is one of the highest worldwide with members from more than 30 Church denominations. The current national President is Sir Professor E.J. Chuta and the National Secretary Mr A.B. Mbamoh.

Okenwa Jideofor Nwatu
Assistant Organizing Secretary of my state council (Enugu state) and an Advanced National Training Officer at the national level in Nigeria. Here at St Andrews I'm an officer in the BB St Andrews Fife Scotland.

Palm in Palm Project – Cameroon

The *Palm in Palm* project was set up in the West African country of Cameroon with the intention of making The Boys' Brigade there self sufficient. In order for this to happen, projects would need to be thought of, and implemented in Cameroon to generate funds for the BB Companies. The main project of *Palm in Palm* is a palm tree plantation which is situated in Mbaw on the North-west region of Cameroon. There are around 500 palm trees on this plantation which will be harvested for the palm oil. This will then be sold, generating money for the Companies, and also to fund the planting of more palms. Another project that has been set up is the donation of several motorbikes which can be used as taxis for members of the BB to use, to make money for them, and the BB.

I was lucky enough to get the opportunity to travel to Cameroon to see these projects, among other things in August 2009. Four other members of BBUK also had the chance to go to see what had been set up, and meet the people involved in the projects. Most importantly, we were able to meet officers and boys in BB Cameroon.

We started our journey on the morning of 2nd August, and arrived in Africa later that evening. We were in the country for two weeks, and in that time we had the opportunity to visit several BB Companies, their communities, and the palm tree plantation. We were also part of the first National BB camp in Cameroon which hosted 300 boys. During the two weeks we met some wonderful and interesting people who made us feel welcome and humbled. There was a lot of travelling involved, but it gave us time to reflect on what we had seen and what would await us at our next destination. The National camp was my favourite part of the trip because it gave me the opportunity to meet some of the boys, and some of the BB Executive, who with all their hard work had managed to put the camp together, and are moving the BB forward in Cameroon. It was also good to pass on some of our ideas for games, activities and songs. The trip challenged us both physically and mentally, but it made us realise how extremely lucky we are, not just in our personal lives, but also in the resources and environment we have for our work in the BB in the UK. Hopefully The Boys' Brigade in Cameroon will one day have similar advantages to carry on God's work.

Benjamin Phillips
1st Redditch, Worcestershire, UK

The BB in Zambia

The 9th Lusaka Boys' Brigade Company (St Andrews UCZ) is a member of The Boys' Brigade of Zambia. Our Company is relatively new as it was founded in 1984. Currently our Company strength stands at 105 members. We are fortunate to have a marching brass band, as well as a bugle band. Other activities include Bible sessions, sporting activities; football, cricket, volleyball and our local games like kankuluwale, may may... etc. Camping and expeditions mark the highlight of our calendar – normally held in southern Zambia near the mighty Victoria Falls (a world heritage site). We also hold the annual inspection, display and awards ceremony and Christmas party about year end. In Zambia the BB was introduced in 1957 however "indigenous" (all races) started in 1965 with assistance of Rev. Christopher Hancock. Currently our national membership stands above 13,000 members with over 50 Companies just in Lusaka, still going strong.

Pile Ray

9th Lusaka Boys' Brigade.

Indian Subcontinent

In the late 19th Century there were a number of missionary-based BB Companies on the Indian subcontinent. One was founded in Darjeeling in 1894 and another at Jalna. In the early 1900s Companies started in Madras, Allahabad, and Bombay. The BB also existed in Sri Lanka (Then Ceylon) until the 1940s. Three Companies were formed in Calcutta between 1897 and 1902. One Company was opened in 1923 at Barisal on the Ganges Delta (now part of Bangladesh). Perhaps the most famous Companies to be formed in India were the 1st and 2nd Dichpalli formed in 1927 and 1932 as part of the Dichpalli Wesleyan Leper Mission Hospital (Victoria Leprosy Hospital) more than ninety miles north from Hyderabad in the State of Andhra Pradesh. This large Company made-up of boys who were being treated at the Hospital, continued long after the time of Indian Independence in 1947, at which time all the other BB Companies had ceased. The Leprosy Mission was supported for many years after 1947 by Methodist Boys' Brigade Companies as part of the Boys' Brigade Branch of the Methodist Missionary Society with an office in Union St. Birmingham.

Today there is no 'BB' in India, but an organisation known as 'Junior Ministry' has been started by the Lutheran Church in a few locations and has become affiliated, like the BB, to the Global Fellowship of Christian Youth. There is a similar organisation in Bangladesh.

Robin Bolton

Dichpalli BB Boys of the 1960s.

Caribbean & St Lucia

The BB came to the West Indies through the missionary Ministers who had an interest in BB and had been boys in the Brigade themselves. That is how the movement got started in the Caribbean.

The first island to have a BB Company is St Vincent and that was only a few years after it was started in UK, I am not sure of the year but somehow think it was 1892. St Vincent is an island in the South Caribbean Methodist District. The island still has active BB Companies functioning in the Methodist Church there. For their 100th year an Eastern Caribbean regional camp was held and at a small round about in the island there is a concrete pillar that has the BB Badge on it to commemorate the milestone.

I am familiar with the work in the Eastern Caribbean islands and that comprises of St Kitts, Nevis, Anguilla, Antigua, Montserrat, Dominica, St Lucia, St Vincent, Grenada, Trinidad, Tobago, Barbados and then these Dutch speaking islands – St Maarten, Curacao, and St Eustatius. All these islands formed one area supervised by a Training and Organising Secretary.

John Edbrooke, of Northern Ireland came to the Caribbean and worked, as Training and Organising Secretary, in the whole area which at that time included Jamaica, Bahamas and the Turks & Caicos Islands. He was sent out by Headquarters in Britain and was stationed in Jamaica.

A world Camp was held in Jamaica in 1958 at which Mr William Henry Mc Vicker attended and after that Mr Edbrooke was sent to co-ordinate the BB in the Eastern Caribbean islands, which he did until he returned to UK in 1962. In 1960 a young BB officer from Barbados, Mr Carlisle Jackson, was given the job of Training and Organising Secretary of Eastern Caribbean which he held until the year 1970.

The BB in the Caribbean has a history of rising and falling and right now it is at a low ebb. With the departure of Mr Jackson there were some lean years but then the Rev Clifton Niles was made Co-ordinator of Eastern Caribbean in 1972 and the movement became very active in all the islands except Barbados. This continued until the early 90's because we were looking for a coordinator as the church had appointed Rev Niles as Warden to the United Theological College of the West Indies in the late 80's.

Some of the highlights were Regional Officers Training Camps, Boys' Camps, the many BB bands, painting of the Methodist School in St Lucia, repairs to schools in Anguilla. A contingent of 30 attended the camp in Scotland to celebrate 100 years in 1983

Each island had an Island council and most of them were privileged to have the Head of State or Governor to be the Patron of the Movement.

Most of the Companies were attached to the Methodist Church but there were a few Moravian Companies and Anglican Companies and at one time St Lucia had a Company in the Roman Catholic Church.

In later years the Anchor Boys movement was added to our BB in the area. The Eastern Caribbean wrote its own Syllabus and programme for this section.

As the area was such a large one an Officers Training School was held each year, for this was an opportunity for each island to be represented and for them to receive training to improve our Companies in each island. This camp moved around the different island and always had at least 100 officers attending. In 1967 a Training of Trainers School was held in Grenada at which certain persons were chosen from each island. These persons were to help with the training of officers in their own island.

ST LUCIA

The Boys' Brigade began in St Lucia at the Castries Methodist church in 1962 with a Life Boy Company. The officers were Barbara Lake, Cynthia and Doris Warner and Kathleen Simmons. The Chaplain with Rev Robert Wakefield. There were 32 boys and soon it was time for some of them to be promoted to a Company. The captain and an officer got the Company moving. Soon there was a vibrant Company of 30 boys meeting every week as well as the Life Boys.

The boys wore the same caps and belts as did those in UK. The Life Boys wore a white T-shirt and navy blue pants with black socks and shoes. The Company boys wore a navy blue shirt and pants with the white haversack, black shoes and socks. Officers wore white shirts and black long pants and the international cap – the ladies wore white blouse and navy-blue skirt and the International hat, and black shoes. (This was the uniform throughout the whole Caribbean area)

Captain George Compton was a very outstanding officer and steered this Company along for many years.

Our programme was very similar to that of Britain for we used the same books and did the Badge system for both sections, with minor adaptations where necessary. Then Life Boys was phased out and we became the Junior Section of the Company, The female officer's uniform also changed to that of the British. Then the boys uniform also went through a change with a choice of either blue or white shirts and navy blue pants- each island would chose which colour shirt to use, caps badges and belt etc; are the same as that of Britain. A bugle and drum band was a highlight in this Company and there was always a march around the town on the way to church parade every 3rd Sunday. The Girls' Brigade also marched with the Boys' Brigade. The BB has been on national parades for the Queen's Birthday. The BB Display was looked forward to and items presented by both boys and officers. Brigade week was usually a fund raising one and so sponsored walks took place – some worked in the supermarkets after school and all Saturday. A special BB Service was held on the Sunday afternoon, at which other youth organisations in the island were invited to attend.

The Rev. Desmond G Mason (chaplain at the time) visiting the 1st St. Lucia Company at Foresterre Church.

Camping was done every year and here the boys did some mountain climbing and volunteer work in which ever part of the country they camped.

Regional camps were held every two years and boys from all the islands in the Eastern Caribbean attended. A different island was chosen each time. It was in 1975 that they painted the Methodist School in St Lucia.

We are very proud that it is through the BB that Allyson Henry joined the Methodist Church and is now Deacon Al Henry serving in the British conference. He always delighted in playing the bass drum.

Barbara Lake

St Lucia history

The Boys Brigade started in St. Lucia in the year 1960 by the Rev. Gordon Wakefield an Methodist Minister from UK, who was then stationed as the Methodist minister on the island.

The Brigade went from strength to strength until the early 70s when it was difficult to recruit new leadership. With the arrival of the Rev. Colin Membery another Methodist minister from the UK, the 1st St. Lucia Company of the Castries Methodist Church was revived with Captain George Compton and Lt. Barbara Lake.

This was the time I came into the Brigade through the influence of Rev. Membery and Barbara Lake who was my head teacher.

The 1st St. Lucia Company grew and we also had a Band which played for many parades and youth activities in the city.

Due to ecumenical talks at the time, our Company was able to suggest to the RC Priest the late Fr. Emmanuel Catty to get a Company going at the Cathedral in the city of Castries.

Right: Picture of Al, age 12, in his Blue & White BB Uniform, he had just joined and had not bought his BB Hat as yet.

Al Henry, Manchester district Battalion Parade 2007.

Al Henry, Gideon, Rev. G. Halley Marville (Chaplain) Andrew Membery (son of the Rev. Colin Membery former Chaplain who revived the BB and got me to join) and two members of the youth group of our Forestierre Methodist Church. What had happened on that day is we had been to Church Parade at 8:30AM and we used to like to meet the girls from our other Methodist Church so used to accompany the minister to the 11AM service. Both Andrew and myself lived near the Church we had gone home to change.

2nd St. Lucia. As the years went on some officers from the 1st St. Lucia gave of their time and started a 3rd St. Lucia Company at Ciceron Methodist Church a few miles from the city.

Within 10 years the 2nd & 3rd St. Lucia folded due to leadership. I was told that in the late 60s there was a Company at Forestirere Methodist Church.

I am grateful to the BB for making me the person I am today. A Christian and a Methodist Minister. I have never left the BB in all those years since 1973. I have served as an officer and chaplain in the 1st & 3rd St. Lucia, 73rd & 80th Birmingham, 57th Manchester and now 28th Leeds.

We praise Him for all that is past and trust him for all that's to come.

Deacon Al Henry
Middleton
Leeds South Circuit

The CariBBean

John Edbrooke, who was BB (UK) Development Secretary, went to the Caribbean in 1953 as BB Organizer for the region. His wife Mollie, who accompanied him, has written specially to us so we can read about their wonderful few years' adventure in the islands.

Our story of the BB in the Caribbean began in 1953, and over the next 10 years our work had taken us all over the islands – starting in **Jamaica** first. Companies rapidly began to grow and the first overseas BB camp in 1958 was held there with boys coming from Great Britain and Ireland. The work of BB got going and I remember such things as The Island Run of **St Kitts**. They were great on island runs! 30 miles around the island. They ran in relays, Junior boys first, then the longer distance for the senior boys. Always a great contest during the year. John explored all the islands, and BB Companies sprang up everywhere. Karl McDonnagh took over as organizer when John made his next quarters in **Trinidad**. All over the islands that we were following down from **Jamaica**, saw many young men take over the various Companies. The islands of **St Kitts** and **Nevis**, **Anguilla**, **St Maarten**, **Trinidad & Tobago**, **Grenada**, **Antigua**, **Tortola**, **The Virgin islands**, **Aruba**, **Virgin Gorda**, and **Haiti** which had one of the finest Companies of 150 boys. Many in **Haiti** had to leave to the USA, Trinidad & Tobago, South America, British Guyana, also Dutch Guyana, French Guyana, Honduras (now Belize) and St Kitts, because of the island troubles with Dictators.

The islands are not really as close together as they seem; it is difficult to keep a united front in the work unless you visit often. I suppose I found it easier as an outsider from Britain, able to be impartial and keep everyone happy. We had 10 really wonderful years and loved the people. And when back in Britain in London during the heaviest snowfall for years we often said to each other "Why did we ever leave the Caribbean?" Actually BB HQ in London had thought it was time for the islands to stand on their own feet.

John died suddenly in 1983, and a few months later the BB in the Caribbean asked me to do visits to many of the islands and encourage training of officers, wherever possible. Boys usually have BB after school – outside on the roadside – inside the school if wet. As there is little in the way of transport they usually walk many miles to BB then home. I managed all the way around the islands despite late planes or 'none until the next day', but boats were helpful – a really great training adventure on my own, and I know John would have liked me to do it. That's now over 25 years ago and many officers and young people will since have had to leave the area, for work or other reasons to the USA, South America, and Great Britain. There were some really excellent officers when I was there, and I am sure there are still strong pockets of activity here and there. I remember one great officer Mr D'Arcy Scott in **Barbados** where Barbara Lake is now. We had a great camp there with180 from the islands around for 10 days. D'Arcy owned a school so it was the HQ of the camp where the officers slept, and the classes were held from 6am rise. Through the day there were all sorts of activities, games, cricket on the beach. The officers came at their own expense, not even being allowed holiday pay, and that meant a lot! D'Arcy and his wife Edna did everything they could to make things easy for everyone. The Governor came and inspected us all! We called D'Arcy the uncrowned *King of Barbados*.

Mollie Edbrooke, N. Ireland.

The BB in North America

There is a terrific history associated with the BB in the North American Continent. The USA's involvement with the Brigade goes back to the first Company in St. Louis Missouri in 1887. The 1st San Francisco Company, under the leadership of the Rev. John Quincy Adams was, from 1889, at the forefront of BB activity. There were 50 Companies on the West Coast, modelled on the British BB, by 1892. In the 1890s the BB really 'took off' in the USA partly due to the efforts of William Smith's friend Professor Henry Drummond a very popular preacher and lecturer. There were thousands of members in hundreds of Companies.

Sadly, the USA of the 1890s was still developing its communication networks, and distance and isolation were the enemies of unified progress. Individual denominations created their own 'Brigades', 'The Baptist BB' and the Methodist 'Epworth Guards' being the most well-known. Individual States favoured their own organisations over any National organisation. Three separate 'National' 'headquarters' developed but in 1894 the Midwest Brigades formed the 'United Boys' Brigades of America' taking the whole movement in the USA into a more militaristic mode and less church-based. Many units were caught up in the move towards the cadet movement, leaving the Brigade. Some notable exceptions to the rule saw individuals such as Jos. H Cudlipp of Pennsylvania and S. F. Shattuck of Neenah-Menasha attempt to breathe new life into the BB in the early years of the 20th Century by returning to the British methods.

The currently successful Neenah-Menasha Brigades in Wisconsin and the remaining Companies of 'The Boys' & Girls' Brigades of America' in the Baltimore area of Maryland are the remaining legacy of the work of Messrs Cudlipp & Shattock and the only 'BB' in the USA today. Many imitators and vestiges of the BB still operate in the USA, Brigade Boys' Clubs, The Christian Service Brigade, The Royal Rangers and the Calvinistic Cadets to name but a few.

In Canada, The Boys' Brigade also arrived in the 1880s and developed along very British lines, the first Company being established in St. John, New Brunswick. By 1892 the BB had spread into Ontario and Quebec. When Lord Aberdeen, the Hon President of the BB in the UK, arrived as Governor General of Canada in the 1880s, the Brigade was further boosted. The 1890s saw a number of Battalions being formed, the largest being in Toronto. Despite a reasonable number of boys, the BB was still operating a relatively small number of Companies and over the twentieth century numbers remained quite static instead of increasing as they were in the 1920s and 30s in the UK. Today there are signs that the BB is attempting to 'Canadianize' itself by operating, for instance, in the Native communities of the Arctic North.

Robin Bolton

Boys' and Girls' Brigade, Neenah, Wisconsin, USA

The mission of the Brigade is, We Build Leaders. Through a seven-year program logic model, Brigade builds character development and leadership skills in youth in 6th-12th grade while proving opportunities to discover new friends and experiences through exciting programs. Hundreds of adult volunteers interact with youth in mentoring roles to reinforce positive morals, ethics, values, and character traits. Brigade provides an environment where youth can grow, explore new opportunities, experience adventure, challenge themselves, and ultimately succeed. A typical two-hour night at brigade consists of an auditorium presentation or workshop, a physical activity, and small group time.

The Brigade's motto, *My Own Self, At My Very Best, All the Time,* fosters positive values, character development, and personal responsibility in youth.

The Object of the Boys' & Girls' Brigade shall be the advancement of Christ's Kingdom and the promotion of habits of obedience, reverence, discipline, self-respect and a spirit that reflects a true Christian life.

As well as the boys' and girls' leadership development programs, we provide an International Program; DNR boater, hunter, ATV, and snowmobile safety classes; run Camp

Woodworking.

High ropes course.

Onaway Island; and have hobby clubs which include Archery, Ceramics, Climbing, Discover Scuba, Downhill Ski, Fly Fishing, Handicraft, Knitting, Model Railroad, Rifle, Sewing, and Small Engine Repair Club.

Onaway Island youth summer camps are an extension of the boys' and girls' leadership development programs. The weeklong camps are open to all boys and girls in grades 6-12 (not just Brigade members), and youth attend from all over the United States and internationally. Camp Onaway is located on the beautiful Chain O' Lakes in Waupaca, Wisconsin. In 2008 the Brigade celebrated 100 years of camping there. Youth are served by volunteer adult mentors whose passion for youth brings creative and fun activities each year. Youth participate in exciting activities ranging from swimming, skiing, competitions, crafts, high-ropes courses, fishing, and much more. One of the camps, Leadership Training Conference (LTC) is an elite Brigade program in its core mission of building leaders and is the ultimate leadership camping experience for youth in 10th-12th grades.

Compiled by Pat Kroiss and Katie Nussbaum

Olivia Boerschinger writes...

Just wanted to let you know that I think the idea of the Facebook group is simply amazing. The Neenah-Menasha BG Brigade may be large, but we're the only one in the US, so I don't ever have a chance to talk to other people in BB.

Last summer we hosted about 30 Scots from a BB in Bearsden who spent part of the summer with us and attended our summer camp. We currently have about 20 Aussies visiting Wisconsin for about a month. I really enjoy having foreign visitors because it is the only way we here in the US can learn about other BB's. Especially since most of the Boys' Brigade Companies in Europe have much more history than ours does here. In June there are 12 people from our Brigade going to Bearsden to visit our friends that came over last summer, should be a blast! I can't wait to see how their BB is run because I hear that ours in the States is run much differently than most.

Just wondering, do you know if the Neenah-Menasha Boys and Girls Brigade is the only co-ed Brigade? Because all I ever hear of is other Boys' Brigades... just curious.

Ed: Olivia, there are lots of co-ed Brigades. Most of the BB in South East Asia is co-ed. The BB/GB in Uganda is the same organisation and the BBUK originally introduced the 'Girls' Association', which is now run as part of the BB.

The boys and girls of the 5th Tanjung Morawa Company. Girls now make up more than 50% of some Boys' Brigade Companies in various countries around the world. Photo: Resien Chiu of Lhokseumawe, Indonesia.

Adam Woodhouse, youth worker from Bradford, England, and the ex-Captain of the 1st Hatfield BB, remembers his time spent at

Onaway Island, USA

Camp Onaway is a $6\frac{1}{2}$ acre island located on The Chain O' Lakes near Waupaca, Wisconsin USA. The Boys' and Girls' Brigade have been camping there since 1908, and I had the privilege of sharing a weeks camp in 2003 with a party of lads from 2nd Witham and 100 American lads! The whole week was based around a tribal setting with senior young people being Chiefs and assistant chiefs, and the leaders being Crows. This is to give the seniors a leadership role to build up skills.

We spent a week on Onaway with each day starting with a choice of jump into a freezing cold lake, or an exercise class to wake you up. My advice was to take the dip in the lake – quick and easy! This was followed by raising the flag before breakfast. The food was fantastic which was all cooked by young leaders and helpers from Brigade. After Breakfast the action packed day began with plenty of time to try basketball, pool, swimming, canoeing, sailing, banana boat rides plus much more.

The atmosphere was very friendly with a big community feel. Each evening you had a sing-along concert, camp baseball game, and BBQ. Also each day there is a team competition and session in the chapel. Some of the great English Brigade camp traditions have made it to Onaway, such as cabin inspection and playing pranks on staff – this one day involved bringing out a leaders bed onto the parade yard and taping his suitcase to it!

Its hard to give you a feeling of Onaway life here but I recommend you take a visit, its well worth it! And a "Hi" to all those at Boys' who in 2003 made me love it!

The Last Post…
My Fellow Brigaders

Last week, my brother Shawn returned from a tour of duty with the United States Marine Corps in Iraq. There are many Brigaders like him who have and are currently serving abroad in times of both war and peace. Brigaders like Jason Foster, Tim "Moose" O'Brien, Travis Fonder, Annette Swanek… and so many others….

The LAST MONDAY of MAY is MEMORIAL DAY. Neenah and Menasha puts on a joint parade through both cities in honor of those who have served and are serving in the US military. This holiday is specifically designed to pay tribute to these individuals and the ideals of freedom and democracy for which they fought. It is an important day and one that we as Brigaders should pay special attention to. So many have given that 'last full measure of devotion' and have sacrificed so much, for so long, for so little. This is the least we can do.

Traditionally, the 1st Wisconsin Battalion of the Boys' Brigade (that's US!) has fielded an entry in this parade. Since before any Brigader now living was born, our Company has MARCHED in UNIFORM in this parade. It is an honor to do so. Robert John Erdman (the very first chore boy) has not missed a parade since he enrolled in the Brigade as a 5th grader – 79 plus years of marching – NOT ONE MISSED PARADE. If you ask the "old folks" in our community they will tell you how impressive the Brigade looked and how much they anticipated the Brigaders rounding the corner. This is what the Brigade motto "Sure & Stedfast" means. It is how we as Brigaders hold the standard high.

There are few opportunities in our lives and culture to do something that has merit and brings honor to our community, our Brigade, our country, our military, our fellow citizens and ourselves. You have a unique opportunity to participate in the Brigade Drill Team. You will work hard, you will develop a skill, you will build and be a part of an elite team, and you will create value and earn respect. You will LOOK SHARP and you will be doing something important. This year as leaders in addition to Adam Waite (Marine) we have Darel Schoening and his wife both retired Lt. Col.'s (Army) for Drill Instructors. They are leading an effort that you as a Brigade should be apart of.

We meet every Thursday evening at 6:00 PM to practice and refine our skills. Those who excel earn the additional honors of being Squad Leaders and Standard Bearers. If you attend practice you become very capable at marching and close order drill. You make at least one new friend and work with very capable leaders. There is FUN to be had as well as a sense of accomplishment and pride. We have also been known to treat the team to DQ when their performance is exceptional.

WHERE: Brigade – 109 W. Columbian Ave. Neenah, WI

WHEN: Thursdays at 6:00-7:00 PM from now till Memorial Day

It matters, so be there.

Jason D Pheifer